"It was the worst kind of nightm
back and we were reeling from a.
to make them pay). This went on for some time, until we were finally ready
to face the whole truth. That's where this book comes in. Ruth Ann is a
wise counselor. She wouldn't let us do the easy thing of either demonizing
the other or ourselves. This helpful book outlines the process she helped us
discover as we embraced a healing path. I heartily recommend it to you."

John Thomas, Director of Global Training, Redeemer City to City

"Childhood examples of and teaching on forgiveness had left me with more
questions than answers. It wasn't until I met Ruth Ann that I discovered another
way. The gospel way! One that has no place for denial of wrong committed.
One that doesn't minimize the damage. And one that waits with patience as we
grapple with our own forgiveness. This is not a quick-fix book; it's an invitation
to a lifestyle. But be forewarned: Batstone's words have a way of blowing up our
preconceived ideas. Of laying the groundwork for the Spirit to begin that deep
heart work that leads to true forgiveness and a new way of living."

Shari Thomas, Founder and Executive Director of Parakaleo

"Profound and practical. In this short study, Ruth Ann draws you to a new
and deep consideration of forgiveness in light of the mercy of a Savior who
has also suffered. As the sacrifice of the cross amazes afresh, prepare for your
own heart to be uncovered. Walk with her through the searching questions
she addresses to the heart, and expect the Spirit's powerful healing work."

Chris and Esther Bennett, Chris is pastor of Wilton Community Church,
north London, and lecturer at London Theological Seminary; Esther is
Committee Manager with Londonwide Local Medical Committees

"We often take a mental picture of those who have hurt and betrayed us the
most and then pull out that picture and say to ourselves, 'I can never forgive you
for what you did to me.' Ruth Ann shows us how the gospel both gives us the
supernatural power to forgive and be freed to love and serve God and others
through the forgiveness he offers us."

John Freeman, Founder, Harvest USA; author, *Hide or Seek*

"Ruth Ann's book doesn't stint or compromise, but bravely cries, 'forgiveness.' She walks us into the wilderness of our hurt and offers us the steel of
real forgiveness. Her book is like enjoying a cup of tea with a wise woman
who has loved a Suffering Servant for a long time. She's the real thing."

Robert Gordon, Marriage and Family Therapist

"J. I. Packer once compared two theologians in this manner. The writings of the first were biblical but 'dry as toast.' The second? Also biblical, but this one 'wrote theology from his knees.' The same can be said of my dear friend Ruth Ann Batstone. It is observable on every page of *Moving On* that she is drawing from a deep wellspring of her own personal struggles with forgiving others. Ruth Ann writes about 'forgiving' from her knees."

Bill Senyard, President of Gospel App Ministries; author of *Fair Forgiveness*

"Nothing is wasted, nothing is lost even when men betray, deceive, and seek to destroy our lives, because God forgives, restores, and redeems the evil. Ruth Ann tells her story of sexual abuse and betrayal with honesty and compassion as through the years she has immersed herself in God's story of grace and forgiveness that brought healing to her life. And now the story goes forth with a message of hope to men and women whose lives have been shattered and broken by the evil done to them."

Rose Marie Miller, Author of *From Fear to Freedom* and *Nothing Is Impossible with God*; coauthor of *The Gospel-Centered Parent*

"*Moving On* helps all of us who get stuck in those nasty cycles of holding grudges and harboring resentment to find the freedom that our hearts and bodies crave. Inspirational, comprehensive, practical, and theologically robust, *Moving On* is a beautifully written primer on forgiveness that can be immediately applied to the heart. Ruth Ann's writing is accessibly transparent. She writes as a seasoned traveler on the road to both give and receive forgiveness and as a seasoned mentor who has led many others to this same freedom."

Drew Angus, Director of Spiritual Outreach, Cancer Treatment Centers of America, Philadelphia, PA

"Ruth Ann Batstone has written a redemptively tricky book. Who doesn't want to read about forgiveness and moving on? While reading the narratives Ruth Ann uses to set the stage of this book, you find yourself reviewing your own betrayals and the 'hall of fame' folks who have caused you significant hurt and sorrow. That is when *Moving On* seeps into exposing your finely honed practice of hardness, bitterness, and self-protection that continues to hold you prisoner. *Moving On* moves the reader past reliving it and offers pragmatic solutions for the reader to learn the work of giving grace and forgiveness wholeheartedly."

Penny Freeman, Counselor with Serving Leaders Ministries and Parakaleo

"Though the title implies a manual on forgiveness, this book offers much more: a broad invitation to live freely in a broken world. Batstone shares richly from a lifetime of honest lament and practical wisdom, enabling us to thrive in the face of suffering. Whether you grapple with deep life-shattering wounds or daily petty irritations, or most likely both, you will find the rare jewel of conviction suffused with hope. I plan to re-read this treasure regularly."

Jennifer Myhre, Pediatrician and Serge Area Director for East and Central Africa; author of *The Rwendigo Tales*

"If you've ever grappled with forgiving someone, you need this book. And even if you haven't, you still need to read *Moving On*; in this sinful world and in the hidden depths of our hearts, forgiveness is always a timely subject. This short book provides God-honoring, practical wisdom that is theologically and emotionally sound. Batstone's clear, concise, insightful writing points the reader to the only source of forgiveness: Christ and the power of the gospel."

Maria Garriott, Resource Coordinator at Parakaleo; author of *A Thousand Resurrections*

"Forgiveness is costly and complex. In her book, Ruth Ann clearly articulates the complicated task of entering the process that offers grace that is counter to our natural desire for justice. From her own life experience as one harmed by someone she trusted, she is now called to walk the path of forgiveness with wounded others. She calls us to look more closely at our own brokenness and to receive grace as we, often reluctantly, are called to the difficult task of offering it to others. She masterfully invites all of us to embrace this path toward transformation found in following Jesus with love and forgiveness. This is a must-read for all who would accept that invitation."

Roy Shirley, Director, Cornerstone Center for Training and Development

"In a world filled with guilt, blaming, and shaming, RuthAnn dares to write what would put her and most every counselor out of business—forgiveness. It's a timely book that simultaneously points people to the greatest Forgiver, Jesus Christ, and then points to our hearts empowering us to forgive others as Christ forgave us."

Steve Resch, Senior Pastor, Walnut Creek Presbyterian Church, Gahanna, Ohio

"Ruth Ann Batstone's book, *Moving On*, is the ultimate healing roadmap for anyone who has ever been hurt or betrayed by someone. Batstone's expert and gentle guidance leads the hurting through their healing journey. She explores crucial milestones such as Christ's faithfulness, the power of the gospel, and understanding forgiveness so that her readers may reach their ultimate destination: Moving on!"

Beth A. Fylstra, Not for Profit and Religious Organization Specialist, Every Little Detail, LLC

"For every person who knows they need to forgive but struggle to do so, Ruth Ann Batstone, seasoned counselor and compassionate guide, shows us the way. With personal stories, sound theology, and thorough research, *Moving On* helps us begin the process of forgiveness and encourages us to make it a lasting lifestyle. Don't miss this essential work on gospel forgiveness!"

Elizabeth Turnage, Writer, Story Coach, Teacher; author of the *Living Story* Bible study series and the Living Story Blog

"Ruth Ann Batstone offers an accessible, much-needed resource that reflects biblically upon foundational issues and gives practical examples. She asks wise questions that bid us to follow Christ down the beautiful, daunting path of forgiveness. Gently and clearly, Ruth Ann challenges us to model him by forgiving even our deepest hurts. Because the unknowing world yearns to see Christ in us, I can't wait to use this book."

Joel Hylton, Area Director for Serge Apprenticeships

"My wife and I first heard Ruth Ann speak on forgiveness years ago. It was like light seeping into the dark recesses of our hearts. Jesus thought forgiveness important enough that when he gave us the Lord's Prayer the one item he commented on further was forgiveness. Ruth Ann's book helps us put Jesus's call to forgive into practice. Thank you, Ruth Ann, for listening to our Teacher."

John Hall, Pastor and church planter

"Though forgiveness is at the core of the gospel message, it's so easy to downplay its centrality. In *Moving On*, Ruth Ann invites us into the heart of God whose grace is found in the most difficult of places. There we learn the extent to which we're forgiven, see the myriad of ways we withhold forgiveness, and discover how we can live daily as those who are forgiven."

Pamela Brown-Peterside, Former Managing Director of Community Groups, Redeemer Presbyterian Church, New York

MOVING ON

BEYOND FORGIVE AND FORGET

Ruth Ann Batstone

New
Growth
Press
WWW.NEWGROWTHPRESS.COM

New Growth Press, Greensboro, NC 27404
Copyright © 2016 by Ruth Ann Batstone

All Scripture quotations, unless otherwise indicated, are taken from The Holy Bible, English Standard Version.® Copyright © 2000; 2001 by Crossway Bibles, a division of Good News Publishers. Used by permission. All rights reserved.

Scripture quotations marked NLT are taken from the Holy Bible, New Living Translation, copyright ©1996, 2004, 2007 by Tyndale House Foundation. Used by permission of Tyndale House Publishers, Inc., Carol Stream, Illinois 60188. All rights reserved.

Scripture quotations marked NIV are taken from THE HOLY BIBLE, NEW INTERNATIONAL VERSION®, NIV® Copyright © 1973, 1978, 1984, 2011 by Biblica, Inc.® Used by permission. All rights reserved worldwide.

Scripture quotations marked MSG taken from *The Message*. Copyright © 1993, 1994, 1995, 1996, 2000, 2001, 2002. Used by permission of NavPress Publishing Group.

Cover Design: Faceout Books, faceoutstudio.com
Typesetting and eBook: Lisa Parnell, lparnell.com

ISBN 978-1-942572-83-1 (Print)
ISBN 978-1-942572-84-8 (eBook)

Library of Congress Cataloging-in-Publication Data
  Names: Batstone, Ruth Ann, 1945– author.
  Title: Moving on : beyond forgive and forget / Ruth Ann Batstone.
  Description: Greensboro, NC : New Growth Press, 2016.
  Identifiers: LCCN 2016025517 | ISBN 9781942572831 (pbk.)
  Subjects: LCSH: Forgiveness—Religious aspects—Christianity. |
    Forgiveness of sin.
  Classification: LCC BV4647.F55 B385 2016 | DDC 234/.5—dc23
  LC record available at https://lccn.loc.gov/2016025517

Printed in United States of America

23 22 21 20 19 18 17 16   1 2 3 4 5

Acknowledgments

It has been an incredible privilege to work on this book, and it is dedicated to the women and men who, with integrity and passion, have shared with me the stories of their struggle to forgive. You have challenged and encouraged me more than you know.

Over many years, I have listened to and read so much of Tim Keller's material that I am often uncertain whether a thought I have is actually mine—or his. It is definitely true that his teaching has been foundational for my personal understanding of who God is and who he invites me to be. Keller has taught me over and over and in so many contexts, how the gospel impacts persons, the world, and my own heart.

Dan Allender, you have challenged the way I understand Scripture and taught my heart to worship the Three in all things. You have given me a biblical paradigm for how suffering can grow and deepen my faith. You are a larger-than-life gospel hero, a brilliant scholar, a clinical genius, and a warm and delightful human being. I have learned from you that in every situation it is appropriate for me to ask myself, "What does it look like to love this person here and now?" I will always be happy that I have been able to know you, share bits of time with you, hear your teaching, and read your books.

Barbara Juliani from New Growth Press has been patient, encouraging, flexible, hopeful, and a resource for all things about writing. I have enjoyed our friendship.

Sue Lutz is a gracious editor who willingly tackled an enormous job. She is humble, kind, resourceful, inspiring, and reassuring. She is strong as well as gentle. I am blessed to work with her. I want to be more like her.

Without the encouragement of Serge and particularly Patric Knaak, this book would not exist. From its origin years ago as a six-week Bible study until its present form, Patric has always, with kindness, said in one way or another, "Just keep swimming."

As a woman, it is a great gift from a loving Father to belong to a cadre of "gospel women." To Tami and Shari and my other amazing and beautiful girlfriends at Parakaleo, as well as treasured lifelong friends elsewhere, like Deb, Carole, and Joyce, thank you for being the good women you are, for loving me through "many dangers, toils and snares," and for inviting me to join you in redemptive struggle.

Virginia, you know who you are. You have loved me and encouraged me to move forward in ministry beyond my wildest dreams. Thank you.

I would also like to thank my children and their spouses, Kristin and Matthew, Todd and Lisa, Jeffrey and Jesse, and Kara and Gerald. I have learned such good things about love and marriage from your examples. You have forgiven me over and over for things both large and small and you may need to continue. Each of you is, to me, a delightful and unique gift from a good God.

And I must thank my grandchildren, Zan, Zoe, Henri, Wilson, Lucinda, Oliver, Liam, Charlie, Gabriella, Fitz, Stuart, and Cecelia. You are the most incredible teens and children that I have ever known. You invite me to dream with you and to see life through eyes where wonder and imagination are always present. I want to thank each of you for teaching me something new every time we are together. Please don't stop. You are treasures of my heart.

And finally, a few words for Stu, the love of my life. There would be no book without your years of encouraging me to pursue my dreams, your hands-on help, and your willingness to step into all kinds of roles so this could be written. Fifty-one years of marriage involves a lot of forgiveness but you have graciously offered it to me again and again. You have also shown me, from your own heart, the real meaning of kindness, honor, tenderness, passion, encouragement, faith, and repentance. I am so very well loved and deeply thankful for the man you are. I love you.

Contents

Introduction

Almost every day there is something I need to forgive. Definitely every day there is something for which I need forgiveness. Forgiveness can be a simple transaction or an extended process. Sometimes it seems effortless, but it can also be complicated and difficult. As you read this book, I hope that you will grow in your understanding of forgiveness. But there is an even more important goal. I hope that you will also begin to have the kind of heart Paul describes in Ephesians 4:32, one that is "tenderhearted" and "forgiving." You have probably already noticed that this isn't natural at all! It certainly isn't to me. But we do have a God who loves us and promises to help us as we ask.

Since you are reading this book, I'm going to guess that you have a reason to be curious about forgiveness. Perhaps you are searching for a way to deal with a difficult relationship with someone you find very hard to forgive. Or perhaps a person you care about deeply is trapped by an inability or even refusal to forgive. I hope that what you read here will be helpful. But please also consider opening your heart a bit wider, so that your growth in forgiveness might lead to more than just the situation that brings you to this book. Forgiveness opens the door to a different way of living where we grow to trust God more, to love others in new ways, and to maybe even begin to embrace life with more wide-open arms.

At the end of each chapter are a few questions about forgiveness. If you like to write in your books, you can answer the questions there. Or you might keep a notebook handy, so that you can answer the questions and interact with what you are reading there. Either way, record things that make you curious, those that don't make sense to you, things that seem encouraging and, certainly, things that you disagree with. Answer the questions or add a few of your own that you might return to later.

An important question to answer as you start this book is this: How do I know if there is someone I need to forgive? The following questions may help you figure that out:

- Are you reading this book because someone you know struggles to forgive? If so, you may also discover some things that are helpful to you. Feel free to investigate them just for yourself.
- Is your own heart struggling with a low-grade issue that doesn't seem to resolve? Are you tired of forgiving over and over?
- Does a trauma or betrayal continue to plague your life and memory? It may be something that seems too overwhelming to even consider forgiving.
- Has a particular relationship caused you harm—a broken friendship, infidelity, divorce, a prodigal child?
- Have you been cheated out of money or had something valuable taken from you?
- Or are you simply but regularly irritated by something that seems insignificant, like your neighbor letting his dog run loose on your lawn?

When we have been hurt, we usually move toward whatever space makes us most comfortable. What is your favorite hiding place?

Do you confront and control,
> run away,
>> find a diversion,
>>> complain to a friend,
>>>> look for something delicious to eat or drink,
>>>>> find a party to attend
>>>>>> or drop out of everything and live in solitude as much as possible?

We called this book *Moving On* to acknowledge that often we feel stuck when it comes to forgiveness. We have been hurt and we don't quite know what to do with that hurt, how to process, how to forgive those who have hurt us, and what moving forward in a relationship does and does not look like. Often, when we struggle to forgive, it can feel as if things are off-kilter, though it may be hard to identify the cause. It just seems like something is wrong with us. We may have a vague sense of uneasiness; we feel like our hearts are unsettled.

But might that out-of-balance feeling be a nudge from the Holy Spirit to search for the source of your distress? What if your unease is his invitation to explore your heart to see what might be tucked away there? Maybe you have become used to feeling the way you do. Maybe you just keep thinking it will disappear. Maybe God is inviting you toward a better plan.

God is infinitely creative in the ways he brings us to himself. Whether we have never known him or whether we have followed him a long time, God is brilliant in arranging a path that leads us to him. Sometimes the road toward forgiveness is straightforward and even short. But it may also be a longer trail path that winds along, with switchbacks, mountains, or even deserts. Whatever course the path takes, the forgiveness you have received through Christ, the deep love and care of the Father, and the power and presence of the Holy Spirit will provide courage and strength as you travel, and perhaps even some surprising joy in the journey.

Forgiveness is often a precursor to change, expected or unexpected. Sometimes we don't know what we need to change or how that change may come about. So as you read, be bold. Ask God to show you what you need to learn and where change might be important. In Psalm 23:3, God says that he will "restore our soul." *The Message* puts it like this: "True to your word, you let me catch my breath and send me in the right direction." This is a great promise. The struggle to forgive can leave us gasping for air, but God's promise in this psalm is a place to breathe and a path that is good. This book is sprinkled through with stories of those who are in difficult situations that call for forgiveness to be both offered and received. As you read, consider what your story is. How does it fit into God's story, and how might forgiveness change and free you to love God and others? Come along and see where the forgiveness path might lead!

CHAPTER 1

Beginning a Journey

Jeff and Christina were at it again. Christina was angry that she was left at home again with their three children while Jeff went to play basketball. She would have to manage dinner and bedtime on her own while he was out with his friends. While he was gone, she spent the time rehearsing what she would say when he returned. She came up with some choice words. Jeff answered back angrily and this was followed by a cold silence between them. But for each of them, their thoughts continued in a steady stream of complaint and negativity.

Jeff was thinking, *I work hard all week. I provide for my family and spend time with them. Why can't Christina see how much I do instead of always being angry every time I do one small thing with my friends? And the things she just said about me! Really?? Next time I think I'll just stay out longer. Who wants to come back to that?*

Christina was thinking, *I am always with the kids. Jeff at least spends time with adults at his job. But he doesn't seem to care about me. No matter what I say, he does what he wants when he wants. I'm going out with my friends and leave him with the kids. We'll see how he feels then!*

It's the same fight that they have had many times before. And they are left with the same feelings and the same distance.

Jeff and Christina are churchgoers who know about the need for forgiveness. But they don't know what it would look and sound like in their relationship.

≈ ≈ ≈

"Life is beautiful," some would say. It can be, but it can also be hard and confusing. Like Jeff and Christina, we can find ourselves in difficult situations where we feel wronged. In response, our hearts move into frustration, thoughts of revenge, fear, numbness, sadness, and sometimes even desperation. Thinking through our responses to these challenges can occupy our minds and drain our energy. But as daunting as it can be to consider forgiveness, it's also important to recognize that the choices we make as we struggle with complicated relationships will impact us emotionally, intellectually, spiritually, and physically. They will have a deep effect on the way we understand ourselves, the way we relate to others and the way we live our lives. It's that important. It's worth the effort.

But even when we know that we have to deal with forgiveness, we often genuinely have no idea how to proceed. There may be blockades that feel impassable; fears that seem unconquerable. It can seem impossible to move forward. We often feel stuck in the same dispiriting ways of relating. But, as one who has faced many of her own blockades and fears, I have written this book to say, "Hold out for hope, because the blessings and benefits of forgiveness are far greater than you may think."

Where Are You with Forgiveness?

When it comes to forgiveness, we have to start by understanding where we are—what we think and feel about the issue, and how we respond to God's call to forgive. So let's begin by looking at the list below. Have you ever said or thought any of these statements? Which ones do you identify with most?

- I don't know how to begin.
- What they did to me happened too long ago. It's better to forget it.
- Why bother? Next week, I'll be angry about the same thing again.
- Some things you just can't forgive.
- I've asked God to help me forgive but nothing happens.
- I've forgiven him, but I can't forgive myself.
- Forgiveness seems unfair. She should pay.
- I can never forgive like God does, so why try?
- Something is wrong with me. Other people don't have trouble with forgiveness.
- I've forgiven her, but I don't like her.
- I won't forgive him until he is sorry he did it.
- I'll probably never see her again, so it doesn't make any difference.
- When someone says that he forgives me, I never know how to respond. I wish people would just say nothing.
- A friend told me she forgave me and I didn't even know what I'd done.
- After what I did to that person, there is no way I deserve to be forgiven. I hope she just leaves me alone.
- It will take me my whole life to pay back the harm I did to my sister.
- I've said I'm sorry. Why do I have to ask him to forgive me and rehash the whole mess?

We all have a history of forgiving and not forgiving, of being forgiven and not being forgiven, so you can probably identify with at least a few statements in this list.

Forgiveness comes in all sizes. We may have to forgive someone for something tiny, like not returning a phone call. We might need to forgive someone for speaking harshly to us (like Jeff). We might need to forgive someone for not understanding our need for help (like Christina). Or we may have to forgive someone for a wrong that harmed us greatly with a lasting impact.

Whether the matter is big or small, it's not long before the need to forgive causes us to face the reality of our own unforgiving hearts. When we experience pain, our hearts may choose many responses that bypass forgiveness. Some let their hearts go numb with a refusal to engage with people, or with hardness and a deep need for control. Some of us respond by being "nicer" on the outside, but only to ensure that we are not hurt in the same way again. Others respond with anger, holding grudges, being critical and bitter, walling off relationships. Some are clever enough to protect themselves by blending in anywhere—or the opposite, by standing out in a crowd. Both can be ways to hide. We can be incredibly creative as we try to protect our hearts from being harmed one more time. Whichever way the struggle and pain of our hearts manifests itself, we can see that forgiveness is usually not our first response when we have been hurt.

But we can't avoid the issue. We may have many ways to bypass forgiveness, but the need for it is universal. Forgiveness is a necessity of life. We live in a world where we need to be free to receive forgiveness and free to offer it. But how did our world get that way? How did *we* get that way?

A Beautiful, Broken World

Our world is staggeringly beautiful but also falling apart. That is also true of us who live in this beautiful but broken place. God created a perfect world. Genesis 1:31 tells us, "And God saw everything that he had made, and behold it was very good." But not long after Adam and Eve were created and given a beautiful garden to live in, they made choices that brought us to where we are today. Adam and Eve decided that all God had given them was not enough; God was holding out on them. Enticed by the Evil One, they took things into their own hands and challenged God's love and care by eating the one fruit God had told them not to eat (Genesis 3). The serpent had slyly asked, "Did God actually say?" challenging the Creator's words. Then he said that if you eat the fruit, "you will be like God" (Genesis 3:1, 5). Eve looked at the tree and considered its fruit. To her, it looked good to taste, so she ate. She then gave some to Adam and he joined in her rebellion.

In that moment of disobedience to God's command, guilt and shame entered the world with a stunning blast. Immediately Adam and Eve had to hide from each other and from God as the fall followed quickly on the heels of creation.

Today we live in a world that is still beautiful in many ways, and we ourselves still reflect—in part—how creation was before the fall. For example, we love beauty and we desire good things. As men and women made in God's image, we long for love and relationship. But we have also been changed by the fall and we, like Adam and Eve, find that our lives have been permanently bent toward independence and getting our own way. We resort to amazing strategies to get what we want or think we need. Those self-centered motivations lead to sinful, harmful words and deeds against God and others. And thus the need to be forgiven for things we've done and to forgive others who have wronged us is present in each of us—it's inescapable. As Romans 3:23 bluntly summarizes, "For all have sinned and fall short of the glory of God."

Without forgiveness, both offered and received, our lives become darker, more isolated, and even further from what we were originally created to be—people who reflect God's beauty, goodness, and holiness and who live in intimate relationship with him. Relationships cannot thrive or even survive in our broken world without the granting and receiving of forgiveness. Jeff and Christina, if they want their marriage to grow in closeness and intimacy, need to know both how to forgive and how to receive forgiveness. As they understand their place in God's larger story—that of Creation, Fall, Redemption, and Restoration—they will also find a way forward in their relationship with each other.

One Great Story with Four Parts

When we struggle personally with forgiveness, it has a way of isolating us from others. In our pain, fear, anger, or hardness, we feel very much alone, stuck in that place with (it seems) no way out. But the fact that the Bible teaches that sin is a universal problem (and thus the need for forgiveness is as well) is good news for each of us, as grim as it is. Why? Because it shows us that our struggles are not unique to us. Instead, it enfolds our lives into the larger story that the Bible tells, the one great story of God's involvement in human history and human hearts. This story is a redemptive drama in four parts: Creation, Fall, Redemption, and Restoration. These four parts can be summarized like this:

1. **Creation:** When everything was as God meant it to be.
2. **Fall:** The tragic intrusion of sin and death, resulting in the pervasive brokenness of all people and everything God has made.
3. **Redemption:** God's promise to redeem creation and his fallen image-bearers through the grace-full work of his Son, Jesus Christ.
4. **Restoration:** The fulfillment of God's plan to gather and cherish a people forever, and to live with them in a more-than-restored world called "the new heaven and new earth."

You might say that first there is Life, then Loss, then Love, then Life.[1]

In Creation, the first act of God's redemptive story, the world in which we live was perfectly created. It displayed beauty, glory, and creativity, all attributes of an amazing God. In the Fall, the second act, sin entered that world, as we have seen, tainting every aspect of creation, including our own hearts. Vestiges of the original world remain, but with the Fall, sin and decay entered our world and marred our own hearts up to the present day. Creation and its inhabitants no longer reflect the Creator as God intended. We see glimpses of what life in this world was meant to be *and* we experience what it has become—persons and places marred by brokenness, separated from God and alienated from each other.

In the third act, Redemption (which we'll look at more closely in chapter 2), God sent his Son, Jesus Christ, to rescue his lost and fallen creation. Jesus did this by living the sinless life that we as human beings were originally intended to live but no longer could. Then he died on the cross in our place, paying the penalty that our sins deserved before a holy God. His sacrifice on our behalf allows all who trust in him to be forgiven for their sins and restored to a relationship with God as his children.

In the fourth and final act of God's redemptive drama, Restoration, those who have been redeemed by Christ will live in a world where everything is right between God, us, and others. Among many other glorious realities, the struggle to forgive will no longer plague us, because there will be no more sin and thus nothing to forgive.

Beginning the Journey

This is the big story that God is telling in the Bible. It is the story that every Christian is a part of. The answers to your struggles with forgiveness lie here. The answers to Jeff and Christina's struggles lie here as well. So with this as our context, where do we begin?

First, think of someone you need to forgive, whether it's for a small thing like a simple oversight or a huge thing that was deeply damaging. It may have happened once or many times. It may have occurred this morning or years ago.

The person (or persons) you need to forgive may have hurt you with angry words, an ongoing conflict, a failed business venture, a betrayal, an abandonment, physical harm, or sexual abuse. The person may be someone you barely know, a family member, or someone you thought loved and respected you.

Sometimes, in God's mercy, forgiveness is the immediate response of our hearts. But it is far more often a process, a journey. It may be long, with twists and turns, or a short sprint. Whatever it turns out to be, pursuing forgiveness will reveal the needs of our hearts and the unimaginable love of the Father for each of us.

A Prayer for David and for Us

At the very end of Psalm 139, David prays a short, intriguing prayer after detailing the amazing and endless ways in which God has searched and known him. He has described how God knows what he will say before he speaks, how he is "hemmed in" by God and cannot go anywhere to flee from God's Spirit. No matter where he is, God will be there. God knew him in his mother's womb while he was still "unformed substance," and all his days were written in God's book before he came to be.

Then he asks God, "Search me, O God, and know my heart! Try me and know my thoughts! And see if there be any grievous way in me, and lead me in the way everlasting!" (vv. 23–24).

After talking about how far God's knowledge of him extends, David still wants more. He did not want anything about him to be hidden from the Lord, so he asks, "Search me, O God . . . and lead me."

As we consider different facets of forgiveness, David's prayer and heart attitude can both be huge helps to us. Often when the Holy Spirit is prodding me to forgive, my response is something like, "I've already done that; don't you remember?" But what if we were willing to pray David's prayer, inviting God to know our hearts, to know our thoughts, to search out our "grievous" ways? Wouldn't a desire to be led in the way everlasting be a great place to begin our journey toward forgiveness?

As we move through this book, we will traverse many types of emotional and spiritual scenery. We may encounter calm seas or hurricanes, glorious mountaintops or dark valleys. We may know the reality of fear, face faltering motivations, and no doubt experience significant fatigue. There may be times when Scripture, other writings, or companions will help us, and other times when we feel very much alone.

Wherever our forward movement takes us, we are sure to experience the wonder that Sam expressed in *The Two Towers*, by J. R. R. Tolkien: "I wonder what sort of tale we've fallen into."[2] At such times, it is a deep comfort to know that God knows us, loves us, and leads us.

Please join this journey with me. Join if you have lots to forgive and you don't know where to start. Join if you have lived through serious harm and feel that you will never really forgive. Join this journey even if you think forgiveness is too hard and not worth the effort. Moving toward forgiveness brings us into new territory and invites our hearts to new growth. It has the potential to open our eyes to the unimaginable love of the Father for each of us. That is the sort of tale I need to fall into. How about you?

Questions for Reflection

1. When someone hurts you and asks for your forgiveness, what is your instinctive response?
2. Are there things a person can do to make it easier to forgive him or her?
3. What things make it harder?
4. What battles might you have to fight in your own heart?
5. What is it like to be forgiven? Think of times when you've hurt someone and the person has forgiven you.
6. Do you ever feel like you don't deserve to be forgiven? Do you want to do something to make it up to the person?

CHAPTER 2

The Foundation for Forgiveness: Being Forgiven

Joe had been working hard on an important presentation at work. He wanted to move his department in a new direction and he had given Sam the job of explaining one part of the new vision. The day before the big meeting, the team gathered to go over their whole presentation. Just as Joe was beginning to realize that Sam had not adequately prepared his part of the project, Joe's boss, Rick, poked his head in the door. Of course, Sam's part was exactly what Rick happened to hear. Joe felt that Sam had made the entire team look bad by being unprepared. Now there would be extra work for Joe to do, but when he tried to talk with Sam about it, Sam became defensive and the conversation did not end well.

Joe felt he had the right to be irritated and his reasons why were clear and specific: (1) The presentation wasn't done correctly, (2) He now had extra work to do, (3) Sam's sloppy work made his whole team look bad, and (4) Sam refused to take responsibility for any of it.

Sam, however, faulted Joe for not being clearer in his instructions or offering help when he knew Sam had so much on his plate.

14

Sam is a churchgoer and recites the Lord's Prayer every Sunday. While it did occur to him that forgiveness might be part of moving forward, he doesn't see how "forgive as the Lord has forgiven you" could help in this situation. He's been trying to avoid Joe.

Now, when Joe runs into Sam at work, he just ignores him. But both of them feel free to vent their frustrations to other team members. Neither thinks about whether offering or receiving forgiveness might be a good thing, or even what a good conversation might look like if they moved away from accusation and defensiveness.

≈ ≈ ≈

In the last chapter, we talked about the fact that forgiveness—both giving and receiving it—is a painful necessity in everyone's life. We also saw why the need for forgiveness is universal. Adam and Eve's distrust of God, their disobedience, and their rebellion were the first sins that entered God's world, and this changed everything. It impacted not only our first parents, but each of us and all of creation, from then until now.

You have probably seen many disagreements played out at work, home, and church like the one between Joe and Sam. And we have all struggled with wrongs done to us (both big and small). The peace that ruled the garden of Eden no longer rules our world today. Our broken relationship with God means that even though we are his image-bearers, we have lost the ability to live in a way that reflects God's character or honors and glorifies him. Instead we focus on protecting, serving, and living for ourselves. No wonder our self-centeredness, fear, pride, and anger make it so easy to sin against others! And it makes it easy for others to sin against us! Joe and Sam are prime examples of image-bearers who have lost their way. Romans 3:10–12 offers this bleak assessment of our situation:

None is righteous, no, not one;
   no one understands;
   no one seeks for God . . .
   no one does good,
   not even one.

No wonder it is so hard to forgive! How could it be otherwise?

God's Rescue Plan Is Activated

The worst part is that we have no ability (or, on our own, even the desire) to remedy any of this. But remember that the Bible tells one big story about God's dealings with human beings, and that story has four parts: Creation, Fall, Redemption and Restoration. The fall has brought God's creation into a pretty desperate situation, but God has never left the story. As soon as humanity fell into sin, God activated the plan that would rescue us from our enslavement to sin and restore us to a relationship with him.

In Genesis 3, God began by telling Satan that someday, one of Eve's offspring would come to crush him and all his evil works (Genesis 3:15). And all through the Old Testament, God promised to send the Messiah, the Savior who would make it possible for our sins to be forgiven.

Isaiah 53 was one of the places where it was spoken of most clearly:

Surely he [the Messiah, the Savior] has borne our griefs
and carried our sorrows; . . .
He was pierced for our transgressions;
   he was crushed for our iniquities;
upon him was the chastisement that brought us peace,
   and with his wounds we are healed.
All we like sheep have gone astray;
   We have turned—every one—to his own way,

And the LORD has laid on him
    the iniquity of us all. (Isaiah 53:4–6)

Through passages like these, we come to understand that only God could do what was needed to deal with our sin problem and our alienation from him. A holy God could not simply ignore our sins or say, "Oh, just forget about them. No big deal." Our sins deserve punishment, and a holy and just God had to exact that punishment. Yet if we paid the penalty ourselves, we would be lost forever, so a loving and merciful God decided to pay the penalty himself on our behalf.

In the New Testament, we meet our Savior when John the Baptist introduces Jesus by saying, "Behold, the Lamb of God, who takes away the sin of the world!" (John 1:29). Jesus was God's Son, sent to live on earth as the Lamb of God, the perfect sacrifice for sin. He lived the sinless life that we were incapable of living and then died as a sacrifice in our place, taking the penalty and punishment we deserved for our sins. John 3:16 says, "For God so loved the world, that he gave his only Son, that whoever believes in him should not perish but have eternal life."

Romans 5:6-8 describes how God was way out ahead of us when he planned our forgiveness. Eugene Peterson captures it well in *The Message*:

> Christ arrives right on time to make this happen. He didn't, and doesn't, wait for us to get ready. He presented himself for this sacrificial death when we were far too weak and rebellious to do anything to get ourselves ready. And even if we hadn't been so weak, we wouldn't have known what to do anyway. We can understand someone dying for a person worth dying for, and we can understand how someone good and noble could inspire us to selfless sacrifice. But God put his love on the line for

us by offering his Son in sacrificial death while we were
of no use whatever to him.

God wanted us to come home, so he made a way for that to
happen. Christ rescues us from darkness and brings us into a
new kingdom of light. Colossians 1:13–14 tell us, "He has delivered us from the domain of darkness and transferred us to the
kingdom of his beloved Son, in whom we have redemption, the
forgiveness of sins."

What Jesus did for us on the cross is sometimes described
as "the Great Exchange." Christ became sin for us and Christ's
record of living, loving, and dying without sin becomes *our*
record. Jesus takes the penalty for our sin and gives us his righteousness. Second Corinthians 5:21 says, "God made him who
had no sin [Jesus] to be sin for us, so that in him we might become
the righteousness of God" (NIV).

A Costly Forgiveness

These are rich truths that a person can spend a lifetime
pondering, but let's consider some specific ways this relates to
forgiveness.

Our sins deserve punishment. They can't be ignored or swept
under the rug. God can't just say "not guilty" when we *are* guilty.
And God *does* wholeheartedly and justly declare us guilty! But
rather than carry out the sentence of death upon us, God sends
his Son, Jesus Christ, to bear the entire weight of our sin and
the punishment it deserves. God's wrath against sin is poured
out on his beloved Son, and divine justice is fully and completely
done. It just isn't done to us. Our sins aren't ignored, minimized,
overlooked, or forgotten. They are paid for completely. There
is nothing left for us to pay, even if we wanted to. And thus the
holiness, justice, mercy, and love of God unite in the sacrifice of
Christ on our behalf.

Because Christ has taken our punishment, God can now forgive us. And because we receive Christ's righteousness, we can be received as his children. This amazing truth—that God himself paid the price for our sins and freely forgives those who come to him in faith—is the foundation for any and all forgiveness in our lives. Our ability to forgive does not originate with us. God's forgiveness came first, and our ability to forgive flows out of the forgiveness we have received from God. It changes our hearts and moves us to forgive others. The gospel is the story of God's pursuit of us when we were his enemies, and the forgiveness and reconciliation he gives us through Christ. As the gospel changes us and enables us to forgive others, we offer them a taste of what God has given us.

So forgiving others begins with understanding our own forgiveness from God through Jesus's death for us. If you have put your faith in Christ as your Savior, then you know what it is like to be forgiven—once and for all, for all sin, past, present, and future. If you are not yet a believer in Christ, consider a God who simply asks you to believe in him and, because of the death of his Son on your behalf, promises that you will receive forgiveness for all of your sins. His forgiveness for you in Jesus Christ will change everything about your life.

If that is true (and it is!) why do so many Christians still struggle to forgive? Why is it so hard for you to forgive? Sometimes it's because we don't understand all that is meant by our own forgiveness before God. We hold on to being right, to looking good in front of others, to being treated fairly because we forget that the verdict is already in.

The Ultimate Verdict Is In

In his booklet, "The Freedom of Self-Forgetfulness," Tim Keller writes about "the marks of a heart that has been radically changed by the grace of God," based on 1 Corinthians 3:21–4:7.[1]

19

Keller says that we all live looking for an *ultimate* verdict" that we are important and valuable. "Every single day, we are on trial. That is the way that everyone's identity works. In the courtroom, you have the prosecution and the defense. We look for that ultimate verdict every day in all the situations and people around us. And that means that every single day, we are on trial. Every day we put ourselves back in a courtroom."[2]

But Paul, the writer of 1 Corinthians, has found "the secret." Paul knows what we also need to know, that the "ultimate verdict is in." "Do you realize," asks Keller, "that it is only in the gospel of Jesus Christ that you get the verdict before the performance?"[3] Usually we think that our performance—in any sphere—will get us the verdict we hope for, but through faith in Christ, it is not the performance that leads to the verdict, it is "the verdict that leads to the performance."

There is a verdict spoken over us in the courts of heaven, and that verdict is "Not Guilty." We know it is true that we are guilty of sin, but where do we get the courage to face that reality? The courage to face ourselves comes from the fact that in heaven we have been declared "Not Guilty" for all time. Romans 8:1 makes it wonderfully clear, "There is therefore now no condemnation for those who are in Christ Jesus." Paul continues in verse 33–34, "Who shall bring any charge against God's elect? It is God who justifies. Who is to condemn? Christ Jesus is the one who died—more than that, who was raised—who is at the right hand of God, who indeed is interceding for us."

Whatever we have done, God no longer condemns us because Jesus has paid the penalty for our sin. God gives us Christ's perfect righteousness as our own.

If today in the courts of heaven someone comes before the Father and accuses you or me—even justly accuses—of sin, there is still no condemnation. Let's say that a person I have hurt comes to God's throne and says, "You need to know that Ruth Ann is guilty of cruelty." Because Jesus has paid the penalty for my sin in my place, there is no condemnation left for me. Jesus took it all.

In God's throne room, we are safe from condemnation. And that safety enables us to look honestly at our own hearts without fear. We can admit what we have done wrong, repent, and be cleansed.

If you have come to God by faith and received his salvation, God's presence is the one place in the universe where you are safe from accusation and judgment. Nothing we have done is minimized, but everything we have done is covered in the atonement of Christ.

Keller is right about verdicts in general and this verdict in particular. We are all on a verdict-hunt. We think and do all kinds of things so that we ourselves or those around us will think well of us, and be impressed by our performance. Joe wanted Rick to deliver the verdict that Joe had done a great job with his team and their presentation. Sam wanted Joe to deliver the verdict that his part of the presentation was great.

We are all on a hunt for ways in which we will have an impact. But, honestly, we cannot live with the kind of consistency required to keep our own hearts or the opinions of others in the "excellent" category. We fail in all kinds of ways, big and small. Though we deserve the guilty verdict that was spoken over Jesus, the One who committed no sin, if we have received God's forgiveness made possible through Christ, the gavel comes down, and the highest court is adjourned,

This decision has great significance for daily life. This is a foundational invitation to live in freedom from having to perform, freedom from worry about what others think, freedom to explore the gifts we have been given, and freedom to love others well, because the "Not guilty" verdict is always there, even when we fail.

On the bookcase next to my desk there is a gavel from a dear friend inscribed with these words: "The Verdict Is In." Believe me, there are days when everything goes wrong, days when I am angry and self-focused and unwilling to care about others. Do I move toward guilty feelings? I do, but by God's sweet grace there are also times when I hold that gavel in my hands and bring it down on my desk with a loud bang as I say out loud, "The verdict is in."

It reminds me that my failures are covered, that my anger is covered, that my lack of loving others is covered by a heavenly verdict. And then, still holding the gavel and wondering at how it can be true, my heart is free to pursue different directions, free to stand under the verdict that Jesus won and love others boldly, even though I know I may make huge mistakes. I am free to think about something besides my own performance and begin again in small ways to put aside my own demands and live for the needs of others. Keller continues:

> Jesus got the verdict we deserve so we could have the verdict he deserved. If you have received God's forgiveness through Christ, then Court Is Adjourned. Jesus lived the life you were too weak to live and died the death you refused to die. If you believe that Jesus has done this for you, not based on anything you have done, at that moment in Christ God gives you Christ's perfect record and you are glorious.[4]

A New Identity, Freedom, and Responsibility

Those who have trusted Christ as their Savior have a new identity. We are now sons and daughters of the King! His forgiveness not only clears my record but also gives me a new sense of who I am. The same God who made me in his image now justifies me and sees me as righteous. Receiving the approval and forgiveness that the gospel provides means that we no longer depend on our performance to be forgiven and right with God. God's forgiveness leads to enormous freedom about who I am before God and before others.

Do you live under this verdict? It means we can rest in what Jesus has done. We can love others because we are covered in the beauty of Christ's perfect life and sacrificial death. It means we are completely forgiven, so we can dare to forgive. In fact, we can risk anything because there is nothing we can lose. If Joe and Sam come to understand that they are living under the verdict of "completely forgiven" by God, they will have the freedom to lay aside their hurt and anger. They will be able to talk through what went wrong, and why, without defensiveness and recriminations.

The same is true for the rest of us. Out of our new identity, we are now free to ask ourselves, "Who are the people I need to forgive?" Here are a few ways to identify them.

- Is there someone you just don't like?
- Is there someone who leaves you with a bad taste in your mouth or a sick feeling in your stomach when you think of him or see him?
- Do you know someone who really irritates you or who consistently makes you feel outright anger?
- Is there a person who makes you inordinately angry when he does some small, annoying thing?
- You are invited to a party and excited to go until you realize that this person has been invited. Suddenly everything changes.
- You hear some friends talking about how interesting this person is. You can hardly restrain yourself (perhaps you don't) from joining the conversation to let the group know what you know about the person.
- Is there a person who regularly triggers your criticism?
- Who might cause a look of disdain to cross your face even though you may say nothing?

You may think of other signals that indicate you have not forgiven. One way that my unforgiving heart becomes apparent to me is when there is someone in my life that I refuse to care about. I can't be bothered; he's someone I am happy to ignore.

Forgiveness in the Lord's Prayer

We have been thinking about God's offer of forgiveness to us from a couple of different angles. Let's revisit it once more in a different context.

> Now Jesus was praying in a certain place, and when he finished, one of his disciples came to him, "Lord, teach us to pray, as John taught his disciples." And he said to them, "When you pray, say:
>
> > 'Father, hallowed be your name.
> > Your kingdom come.
> > Give us each day our daily bread,
> > and forgive us our sins,
> > > for we ourselves forgive everyone who is indebted to us.
> > And lead us not into temptation.'" (Luke 11:1–4)

Have you ever wondered about those words, "Forgive us our sins, for we ourselves forgive everyone who is indebted to us"? If you pray this prayer, inevitably it will lead you to ask yourself if there is someone you have not forgiven. Or perhaps you might think, "I don't always forgive. Does that mean that I'm not forgiven?" The prayer may prompt us to ask, "Who have I forgiven so that I can ask God to forgive me?" But can we really compare the way we forgive to the way God forgives?

Most Bible scholars would say that the use of the word *Father* indicates that the person praying is a believer, one whose sins have already been forgiven because he trusted in Jesus's death to pay for his sins. The prayer seems to imply that being forgiven leads a person to forgive others. So if you realize that there *is* a person you haven't forgiven, it should at least lead you to ask if and how you have been impacted by God's forgiveness.

The Link Between Forgiven and Forgiving

Why does Jesus link the forgiveness we receive to the forgiveness we offer? Jesus is not saying that God will only forgive us if we forgive others. He is not saying, "If you forgive, you will be forgiven." That would mean that we can "earn" God's forgiveness by our good works, and the Bible makes it clear that this is not something we can do.

God's forgiveness doesn't come to us because of our own efforts to deserve it. Paul reminds us, "By grace you have been saved through faith. And this is not your own doing; it is the gift of God" (Ephesians 2:8). Also, Ephesians 1:7 says, "In him we have redemption through his blood, the forgiveness of our trespasses, according to the riches of his grace." So Jesus is not saying that you will be forgiven *because* you forgive others. It is the other way around! Jesus is laying out a pattern: First we receive forgiveness from him and then we offer forgiveness to others. Jesus's death to pay for our sins made it possible for us to be forgiven. The result is that, even as sinful people, we can also forgive others. That is why the Lord's Prayer reminds us of both these things on a daily basis. We need to be forgiven. We need to forgive.

The everyday nature of receiving and giving forgiveness is as basic and essential as our daily need for food. Each day as we ask God, "Forgive us our sins," we are admitting we are sinful and guilty. Sometimes we are guilty of the sin of not forgiving others, but the more we realize how much God has forgiven us and how he *continues* to forgive us, the more our hearts are softened over the things we might otherwise refuse to forgive. Forgiveness leads to forgiveness. So if you want to be able to forgive others, the first question to answer is, "Have I been forgiven?"

When We Don't Want to Forgive—a Flashing Warning Light

Forgiveness is a crucial issue for us, but it can be difficult. When I realize (yet again!) that I don't want to forgive someone who has hurt me despite the Father's forgiveness of me, my own hard heart is revealed. My inability to forgive reveals that I have lost my connection to my heavenly Father's forgiveness of me. Instead of living out of my great forgiveness in Jesus, I have put my faith in something else—my actions, my record, my reputation, an "eye for an eye" system in which I think I've got the upper hand and want my "rights" exercised. I want justice done to someone who has harmed me. I'm willing to trust that type of justice instead of (and at the expense of) God's mercy.

The lack of forgiveness in our own lives should be like a flashing light saying, "Warning. You have lost the gospel of forgiveness freely granted and freely offered. You are choosing a 'judge by your actions' paradigm that you could not live up to yourself. Continuing to follow this path means rejecting the Savior who can save you." This warning removes me from my self-appointed role as judge, convicts me of my sin, and again reminds me of my need for mercy, the amazing mercy I have already received.

At the same time, it is important to remember that, because of the foundation of the gospel and God's enormous grace to us, he is incredibly patient with our heart struggles. He invites us to obey him without demanding that we follow a certain timetable. But he continually invites us to himself. He knows that we are dust, that our hearts are hard and stubborn, and so, as a gracious Father, he uses mercy as an invitation to repentance and change.

The good news is that the One who loved us and gave his life to ransom us from the kingdom of darkness offers us forgiveness. Ransom can be defined as "to deliver especially from sin or its penalty; to free from captivity or punishment by paying a price."[5] It cost God a great deal to ransom us! By contrast, living without receiving forgiveness from God or others and without offering forgiveness to others can trap us just as a prisoner or slave is held captive.

As followers of Christ, we are God's beloved children and so, when our hearts become entangled and immobilized by not forgiving, he pursues us with the same kindness he offered when we came to faith in him. Paul says in Romans 2:4 that "God's kindness is meant to lead you to repentance." In this way, God makes forgiveness the foundation of our relationship with him and then asks us to forgive others. When we first come to know God through Jesus, we admit to God that we need forgiveness for sin. This humbling admission leads to joy and freedom. The burden of guilt and shame is lifted. And then we are free to offer others a taste of what we have received.

Questions for Reflection

1. Have you received God's forgiveness?
2. How has the forgiveness God freely offers you affected the way you think about forgiving others? If it hasn't affected you, what might be blocking its impact?
3. Have you experienced forgiveness from others? If your answer is yes, list some things others have forgiven you for, both one-time events and repeated offenses. If your answer is no, what might be blocking your experience of being forgiven?
4. Have you had to forgive others? Describe a time when you forgave someone and its impact on your heart and the other person's heart.
5. What are some ways that knowing how much God has forgiven you might change your perspective as you attempt to forgive others?

CHAPTER 3

First Steps toward Forgiveness

Paul and Tina's seventeen-year-old daughter Rory told them that she was going to a friend's house for a sleepover. She assured them that her friend's parents would be there. Usually Paul and Tina made it a point to check out the details, but this time they assumed (wrongly) that Rory was telling the truth. A few days later, they learned from Rory's friend's parents that they had gone out that evening and a whole group of teens (including Rory) had used their house for a party. Rory denied everything and claimed that Paul and Tina were wrong for "not trusting her." Paul and Tina were furious. This wasn't the first time that Rory had been caught in a lie. Almost every week, they learned about something she had done that they'd known nothing about. They were tired of being lied to, tired of having to "police" their daughter and, most of all, exhausted from worrying about her all the time. Paul said to Tina, "I know it's wrong to feel this way about your own child, but I can't even talk to her right now." Tina completely understood. They knew that God wanted them to forgive people, but they didn't see how this applied to the situation with Rory. They certainly didn't know what it would look like.

≈ ≈ ≈

In the last chapter, we saw how God dealt with our need for forgiveness. Our sin and rebellion against God earned us the punishment and the penalty of death, something we could never pay except by being separated from God for all eternity. Romans 6:23 sums it up: "The wages of sin is death, but the free gift of God is eternal life in Christ Jesus our Lord." Jesus's atoning death on our behalf paid our sin debt and thus is the foundation for our forgiveness by God.

When we trust in Christ, we acknowledge our complete inability to earn God's favor or to somehow make up for our sin, repay God for his mercy, or in any way rely on our own performance to be made right with God. When we receive God's forgiveness through Christ by faith, it brings a deep change in our hearts. "If anyone is in Christ, he is a new creation. The old has passed away; behold, the new has come" (2 Corinthians 5:17). This heart transformation is most clearly demonstrated, Jesus taught, in our willingness to forgive those who sin against us. Jesus taught about this in a powerful story in Matthew 18, The Parable of the Unforgiving Servant.

How Much Must We Forgive?

In the verses that precede the parable, Jesus was teaching about his Father's love for those who are lost (vv. 10–14) and how to restore a person who has fallen into sin (vv. 15–20). Peter then asks Jesus a question. "Lord, how often will my brother sin against me, and I forgive him? As many as seven times?" Jesus said to him, "I do not say to you seven times, but seventy-seven times" (Matthew 18:21–22).

Since Jesus has just taught about the discipline and restoration of someone who has sinned (vv. 15–20), Peter was asking about our responsibility as believers not just to confront and restore a sinner, but also to forgive someone who directly sins against us. He seems to (rightly) anticipate that Jesus would not want us to seek revenge, but he also seems to assume that eventually there should be consequences to our actions as justice is pursued. Since he knows that Jesus typically views the standards of the religious leaders as deficient, he takes the accepted rabbinic teaching that one is obligated to forgive someone three times for a repeated sin and generously raises the number to seven times. But Jesus responds, "Not seven times, but seventy-seven times."

What Jesus makes clear in the parable is that both the religious leaders and Peter were operating on a faulty assumption. That assumption, which is also the natural inclination of our flesh, is that sooner or later, people should get what they deserve, based on their actions. Peter was more generous in the number of times he was willing to forgive, but he was still following the same paradigm: Sooner or later, we can stop forgiving someone because he no longer deserves it. Though we want mercy extended to us by God indefinitely, we expect justice when we deal with everyone else. That's certainly how Paul and Tina were feeling about their daughter Rory. As much as they loved her, they were exhausted by her bad behavior. If they had been standing with Peter, talking with Jesus, I think they would have had much the same question: "How many times do I have to forgive?" But in the story that Jesus tells, he offers a different paradigm for forgiveness, one based not on how we have been treated by another human being, but based on how God has treated us.

The Parable of the Unforgiving Servant

23 "Therefore the kingdom of heaven may be compared to a king who wished to settle accounts with his servants. 24 When he began to settle, one was brought to him who owed him ten thousand talents. 25 And since he could not pay, his master ordered him to be sold, with his wife and children and all that he had, and payment to be made. 26 So the servant fell on his knees, imploring him, 'Have patience with me, and I will pay you everything.' 27 And

out of pity for him, the master of that servant released him and forgave him the debt. [28] But when that same servant went out, he found one of his fellow servants who owed him a hundred denarii, and seizing him, he began to choke him, saying, 'Pay what you owe.' [29] So his fellow servant fell down and pleaded with him, 'Have patience with me, and I will pay you.' [30] He refused and went and put him in prison until he should pay the debt. [31] When his fellow servants saw what had taken place, they were greatly distressed, and they went and reported to their master all that had taken place. [32] Then his master summoned him and said to him, 'You wicked servant! I forgave you all that debt because you pleaded with me. [33] And should not you have had mercy on your fellow servant, as I had mercy on you?' [34] And in anger his master delivered him to the jailers, until he should pay all his debt. [35] So also my heavenly Father will do to every one of you, if you do not forgive your brother from your heart." (Matthew 18:21–35)

There are many things to learn about forgiveness from this story. Consider the debt. When the king forgave his servant, he didn't deny that a debt existed or pretend that everything was okay. There is a vast difference between a debt being forgiven and a debt being ignored. This debt was enormous, since a talent was the largest monetary unit that existed (about twenty years' wages for a laborer) and 10,000 was the largest numeral for which a Greek word existed. Some scholars estimate that 10,000 talents represented 300 tons of silver. For all intents and purposes, it was an infinite debt that the servant could never repay.

The King's Mercy

Yet the servant pleads for patience, assuring the king that he will pay the entire sum. The king knew he could not, and his heart was moved in pity toward the man—perhaps even pity for his lack of realism—and the king released him, repaying the debt with his own funds. The servant's debt was forgiven.

What are the parallels for our lives? Our debt to God (who is represented by the king) because of our sin is also infinite, and beyond our ability to pay. But while the servant's debt could be handled with money, our sin debt can only be settled by Christ's atoning death on the cross (Hebrews 9:11–28; 1 Peter 1:18–19). As a holy God, God had to punish sin. It could not simply be forgotten or ignored. As theologian John Stott put it:

> At the cross in holy love God through Christ paid the full penalty of our disobedience himself. He bore the judgment we deserve in order to bring us to the forgiveness we do not deserve. On the cross, divine mercy and justice were equally expressed and eternally reconciled. God's holy love was satisfied.[1]

The king had every right not to forgive the debt, but he chose to do so. Likewise, God in his mercy chose to pay the infinite debt we owe him due to our sin, even though he would have been perfectly just to punish us and send us to hell. The servant's plea for patience only highlights the king's generosity in forgiving the debt completely. But this act of mercy cost the king a great deal. He took a huge financial loss, but set the servant completely free. Our forgiveness and release from the debt we owe God cost him even more: the life of his dear Son.

The Servant's Heart Revealed

But the story is not over. As he leaves the king's presence, the servant encounters another servant who owes him a much smaller debt of 100 denarii (a denarius was a day's wage for a laborer). It is a real debt, but very small compared to what the king had forgiven him (100 denarii compared to 60 million denarii). However, the unforgiving servant did not see it that way. He angrily demanded payment and choked his fellow servant, throwing him into prison as a debtor. Despite the debt he had just been forgiven, and despite the echo of his own plea to the king in the servant's plea to him, he has neither pity nor mercy. How could he do this?

Although the king's forgiveness of the debt was offered with kindness and pity, it seems that the servant accepted it with a far different attitude. Apparently he really wanted to believe that he would and could pay the king back. I've even wondered if he was counting up what the other servant owed him while he was standing in the king's presence. He didn't really understand or accept how much he needed the king's mercy and generosity. He had been pulled back from the brink, yet that is where he sent his fellow servant. He had been offered mercy, but he was unchanged by it. He wanted justice for the servant who was just like him and he pursued it with vengeance.

We are so like this! When we come to Christ, we are often overwhelmed with his mercy and grace. But we walk away thinking about how we will pay him back by our good life and obedience. And before we know it, we are demanding payment from someone who owes us a debt, someone just like us, who cannot do what we could not do. It is the natural response of our fallen hearts.

Meanwhile, the other servants are deeply upset by the unforgiving servant's actions and they tell the king all that has happened. The king is furious. He calls the servant wicked and challenges him: "Shouldn't you have had mercy on your fellow servant just as I had on you?" (NIV). He was angry not just that the servant had not cancelled the debt; he was angry that the servant had not had a change of heart and attitude after what he had done for him. He ordered that the servant be put in jail and tortured until the debt was paid in full (v. 34).

The Struggle to Forgive

This deeply sobering warning ends Jesus's parable. If we do not forgive others from our heart, we will suffer the consequences of our hearts never having been changed by Christ, because a refusal to forgive others means that we are still living a life that is based on a self-righteous demand for justice. It reveals a heart that has not been convicted of sin or humbled in gratitude by the mercy of God in Christ.

Jesus very much wants us to take this story to heart, because we can easily lose sight of the gospel of grace when faced with the need to forgive others. But forgiving others is one way the gospel is rooted deeply into our hearts, as God's Holy Spirit empowers us to take the forgiveness we have received and share it with others.

Certainly, we need the Spirit's help to deal with the pain involved in forgiving. Let's say that someone has harmed you. There might be a literal debt, where someone has taken money or property from you or cheated you in some way. Forgiving almost any debt can be painful because of the literal cost to you, plus the emotional cost involved in paying a debt that isn't yours. When we choose to forgive—absorbing the loss and paying the debt on another's behalf—the cost may well involve grief, sadness, and suffering. Certainly Paul and Tina are facing the costs involved in forgiving their daughter Rory again and again. They are hurt by her attitude toward them, her disregard of the rules that are meant to keep her safe, and by the insults she is so willing to heap on them when they try to correct her.

The same is true for each of us. When someone harms us physically, emotionally, or spiritually, we feel pain, whether the pain comes from

- a physical wound
- rejection or condemnation

- someone who treated you with coldness, avoided you socially, excluded you—perhaps even as a family member or a close friend
- being handed a platter of self-righteous judgment for something you did
- experiencing the sting and grief of being used by someone for his or her own pleasure, relationally or physically, in the devastation of sexual abuse.

In all of these situations, there is pain involved. Part of the pain may be that you were left lonely, isolated, and confused by your anger. You certainly could be angry at how you were harmed, angry toward the one who harmed you, or the one who didn't protect you. You may even be tangled in a hard struggle with God for allowing it to happen. Anger is a part of grieving. Our grief may involve facing the reality that our world is not safe or free from pain, even though we belong to God.

Despite all this, the story in Matthew tells us that the deeper truth remains: we are called to forgive as we have been forgiven. In our struggle to do so, we will either pay the debt ourselves by offering forgiveness or we will make the other person pay by finding a way to punish him or her for what has been done. In our worst moments, we may even want to cause pain in return. Our choice will reveal what we are doing with the forgiveness that God has offered us.

Indicators of an Unforgiving Heart

When I forget the gospel and what Christ has done for me, the first, instinctive movement of my heart is to try and extract payment of the debt from the other person—to make the other person pay for what he or she did to me. Here are some indicators that show me when I am expecting someone to pay for what he or she did to me—to pay the debt owed to me:

- What was once a warm relationship suddenly becomes chilly or even cold.
- I desire to control everything I can about that person. I become demanding when we are alone or around others, though I may be quite subtle about it.
- I find my heart overflowing with criticism and complaint; with a demand that the person acknowledge every single word she used to harm me. I am skilled at doing this without uttering any words at all.
- I carry out small acts of revenge toward the person. They may be tiny things that leave no mark or cause no more pain than a pinprick, but they are, for me, sweet revenge.
- When the opportunity arises, ostensibly out of a deep concern for the person's spiritual well-being, I attack her reputation by warning others to be "careful" of her.
- In my heart, I root for her to fail or I gossip to others in a way that sets her up for failure.
- When she does fail, I internally celebrate how much she deserved what she got.
- I spend lots of time remembering her past and present wrongs, thinking, "Here is the proof that everything I ever thought about this person is true."[2]

If I believe that someone owes me something because of what she has done against me, I am looking for payment and my heart moves toward:

- Judgment: "I would never do something like that."
- Accusation: "She is really mean and cruel."
- Deep resentment: "She cannot be trusted and I now refuse to trust others."

As these feelings intensify, my heart becomes hopeless. I refuse relationships and refuse to trust God or others. My commitment to "I'm going to make sure no one ever hurts me like that again" grows deeper and deeper in the core of my heart. But there is no faith in that. There is no gratitude to God for what he has done for me in Christ. There is no trust that he can take the evil that has been done to me and bring healing and help to me, in his own way and timing, as I believe the gospel for my life and seek to forgive as he calls me to.

The Path to Forgiving

In the Matthew story, the king paid down the huge debt with his own funds. He took the loss. When people sin against us and owe us, it is hard to stop expecting them to pay for it—to make up for it—and even harder to be the one who pays the debt for them instead. But that is what we are called to do, for our own sake and for the glory of the God who loved and forgave us. As I face my struggle to trust God and respond to the call to forgive, God directs me to do several things that will help me to forgive.

- I look at my own unforgiving heart and ask a very difficult question: "Are there any ways that I might be like the person who hurt me?" Looking at the ways my own sin put Christ on the cross gives me a more honest picture of myself and the debt I owe to God.
- I confess my hardness of heart to God. I ask the Holy Spirit to show me what my heart is really like, and to bring repentance to the hard, stony places that he clearly knows about.
- I begin to "pay down the debt" by acknowledging the sadness and hurt that the person's sin has caused me, and I do not demand that he repay me for my pain or make it up to me. Yes, my heart will ache. Deep hurt may require deep grieving. But I will ask God for the strength to absorb the loss and forgive. And I will ask for faith to remember his promises to me in Christ and

to believe that he will be working for my good as I follow him by faith.

- One of the biggest costs of paying down the debt is to refuse to continually rehearse the person's sin over and over in my mind. Another is to refuse to rejoice in any pain the person has to suffer so that he is in pain as I am. Instead, I remember that God is gracious, and ask that his grace would soften my hard heart so that I can forgive and release the person to God.

Our forgiveness of others can only take place when we are changed by the forgiveness we have received from Christ, relying on his power to offer others what God has given us. Forgiveness means releasing guilty persons from the punishment they deserve for their sins against us, because the Father has released us from the punishment we deserve for our sins against him. Our ability to forgive comes only from the forgiveness we have received; we cannot forgive in our own strength or efforts. But an unwillingness to forgive indicates that we are not receiving and living out of God's forgiveness; instead, we are living on the basis of justice and what is "owed" to us, not mercy.

When we forgive others, we are not denying or minimizing the harm they have done, but we are applying the power and promises of the gospel to our own pain first, for healing, strength, and hope. Then we can offer that same hope and help to others by forgiving them. That kind of gospel-motivated forgiveness reflects the face of the Father to those we forgive, and draws us closer to him at the same time.

How about Paul and Tina? As they reflected on these truths, they begin to have hope for themselves and for Rory. They remembered that they too were once far from God. They remembered all of the ways that they continue to sin through their lack of love. And they remember that Rory has no power to change herself. They didn't stop trying to keep Rory safe from her own bad choices (that was the job God had given them as her parents), but they were able to respond with kindness and concern instead of anger or a cold avoidance. Rory noticed. She didn't change overnight (who does?), but even she could see there was something different about the way her parents were treating her.

How about you?

Questions for Reflection

1. How do you suppose Peter thought Jesus might answer him about how often we are to forgive? How do you think he felt when Jesus did respond to his question?

2. What do you think the king was thinking when he forgave the servant's debt? What do you suppose was going on in the (first) servant's heart?

3. What are some things in your life that are part of the debt Jesus gave his life to pay?

4. We can spend a lot of time listing our best qualities to others, to ourselves, and even to God, to avoid facing the reality that we are still sinners, though we are forgiven. Perhaps you don't declare your innocence before God, but what kinds of things go on your "I'm still a good person list"?

5. What kind of loss do you imagine you will have to deal with as you forgive?

6. Does the idea that it may cost you something to forgive trigger any alarms in your head? How does this parable help you to willingly move toward more pain?

CHAPTER 4

My Story of Forgiveness

Our stories of forgiveness are often complex and multi-layered. There are many ups and downs as God calls us into deeper trust and dependence on him. I would like to share some of my own story with you. It centers on an area of my life where I have had to struggle with forgiveness over many years. I hope it will help you understand your own journey.

I am an only child. When I was ten years old, in the sixth grade, my father died after heart surgery. He had lived his very short thirty-eight years pouring himself out as a minister of the good news of the gospel. In the last months of his life, he traveled to Ireland to preach, and God sent the Holy Spirit into the hearts of many people, who came to understand the message of God's grace more fully or for the first time put their faith in Christ.

My father had a damaged heart valve after a childhood bout of rheumatic fever. At the time, the only available treatment was very rudimentary and risky. Today, there are many options for dealing with this problem, but for my dad there was only the choice of a dangerous operation.

The night before he went into surgery, Christians across the United States and abroad spent long hours—some the entire night—in prayer, asking God to spare my father's life and ministry. I believe they were prayers of faith. But God said no and took my father home to heaven.

There are some things we will never understand in this life and for me, my father's death, so early in his life and in mine, definitely falls into that category. God's answer to those prayers changed my life.

A Changed Life

I remember with excruciating detail being awakened in the middle of the night, knowing something was wrong, and having my mother tell me that my father had died.

Perhaps you have seen the movie, *Incredibly Loud and Extremely Close*. It is the story of how a young boy, Oskar, deals with his grief after his father dies in the World Trade Center collapse on 9/11. I was surprised at the deep impact that movie had on my heart more than fifty years after my father's death.

I remember that awful feeling of loss and emptiness. The realization that my father was gone and would never be back, and the pain that was beyond understanding. I remember doing some of the things that Oskar does in the film, trying to make sense of something that is impossible to understand. Even as I write this, I can feel the sadness that comes from realizing that I never had the opportunity to really know the amazing man who was my father.

I am still learning about the impact my dad's death had on my life, but I believe that in the years following his death, God pursued my heart in an unusual way.

In the next ten years, I grieved the loss of two sets of grandparents, an uncle, an aunt, and a close eighteen-year-old friend. Grief became familiar to me. I understood it. Looking back, I have often wondered if God was not even then shaping my heart toward a specific calling as a counselor.

But my father's death left a huge vacuum. Adolescence was looming and during that time, some men, close friends of our family, moved into my life in wonderful ways. Hamburgers, milk shakes, games . . . and they taught me to fish.

If you knew me well, you would know that I still love fishing. Catching little croakers and sunfish with my grandkids. Fishing for albacore tuna off the coast of California until my arms couldn't hold the rod or bring one more fish into the boat. Standing on the stern of a boat in Alaska and attempting to harpoon the huge halibut on my line. Or sailing in the Virgin Islands recently and seeing the mahi mahi I was trying to reel in jump completely out of the water to display all of his gorgeous colors.

The men who came alongside me when I was eleven years old taught me to dig for big juicy night-crawler worms. They taught me how to bait my own hook, how to take the fish off the hook, and how to clean it afterwards. I have sweet memories of sitting on the edge of a pond on a summer evening, watching . . . waiting for that red and white bobber to go down. It was an idyllic experience—a picture of innocent pleasure and delight.

Betrayal

But one of the men who came alongside after my father's death, someone I completely trusted, also sexually abused me.

This man's sin against me meant that he incurred a debt. He had taken something from me that he had no right to take. What was the debt? What did he take from me? Here are some ways I was impacted.

1. My childhood innocence was stolen and replaced with shame. I assumed that the fault was mine and I began to feel dangerous to others and myself.
2. My ability to trust was damaged. On the one hand, I responded by trusting other unsafe persons, which led to further abuse. On the other hand, I learned how to make life work without needing to trust anyone.

3. My safety had been breached. I was no longer safe even among family friends, and fear became a permanent resident in my heart.

4. Finally, my ideas about God were damaged and confused. I began to question his love and his goodness, and I felt alone and abandoned by him.

Facing the Damage and the Debt

When we choose to forgive, we need to understand the extent of the debt owed to us by the person who wronged us. It is an important step, because forgiveness means that *we* are paying down the debt that the other person owes us, rather than having that person pay for what he did.

When the time came that I began thinking about forgiveness, I had to begin by realizing that it was not my debt. I was not the one who had wronged someone else. The debt belonged to this man, a friend of the family.

And as I thought about paying down the debt—absorbing the loss and damage myself instead of making this man pay—I had to begin by facing the harm that had been done to me. I had to be willing to grieve what he had destroyed.

I experienced times of anger because I had not been protected and because someone who should have been safe did so much harm.

I realized that I had experienced a great loss. It changed me in ways that are still sometimes evident in my life. There was no way to deal with this huge debt without suffering.

Encountering Grace and Going Deeper

My time to face the damage and the debt did not really come until many years after my abuse, when I went through a course offered by Serge (then World Harvest Mission). I began to understand the reality of the gospel in new ways. As I studied through the Sonship course, God came with incredible power and opened my heart to the reality of his grace. And the more we grow in grace, the more we are able not only to *see* the sin in our own heart, but to feel deep repentance for what we find hidden there. Paul says that it is God's "kindness" that leads us to repentance. His grace enables us to be honest about who we are, how we make life work on our own, and how we worship many other things besides God himself.

One realization that came to me during that course was the truth that in some ways my heart was a lot like my abuser's heart. I saw my sense of entitlement, my selfishness, my willingness to use others to get what I thought I needed. Make no mistake, this man's debt was huge, but so was my own. I had to go to my husband and my children and confess to them the ways in which I used them for my own benefit.

However, it was still a challenge for me to forgive. Denial has layers. For a long time I could acknowledge that the abuse happened, but when I had to acknowledge that there had been a deliberate, planned seduction on my abuser's part . . . I came undone.

I had to look at the gift he gave me—spending time with me after my father died, inviting me into relationship with him—and see that all this had been tainted with his plan to seduce me. When I realized the enormity of how good things had been horribly distorted and I had been deliberately deceived, I simply did not know what to do.

And there are other ways in which my story is a confusing one. The man who harmed me was an otherwise kind and tender person. He was an elder in his church and I have clear memories of seeing him on a Saturday evening with his Bible in his lap, preparing for worship on Sunday morning.

He was married to a woman who was difficult, angry, perhaps even bitter. But part of the love my family had toward this man came from the fact that he treated his wife with love, tenderness, and compassion.

In some ways, it would have been easy for me to write off what had happened, to pretend it never existed, to call it something else. Perhaps I could simply excuse the abuse as some kind of indiscretion or lack of control on the part of a sad, lonely man. But that would not have been forgiveness. Forgiveness is not about denying what happened.

Forgiveness is not about forgetting, either. Thirty years later, the harm that was done can still surface in a new way so that I feel its effects all over again. When that happens, I have to forgive again—the past wrong and the present damage.

Some time ago I was visiting in the area where the abuse occurred. Seeing visual, spatial reminders brought back the terror of those moments. And it made me weep for that little girl who had been so harmed. I had to ask God for grace to forgive yet again. Then my forgiveness was not so much about the raw pain but about the long-term damage to my heart, about the tenacious tentacles that can interfere with my ability to trust and love God and others.

As I've said, life is complex, because there is another part of the story too. Our life stories can feature many different twists and turns. Not many years ago, someone in the family gave me a gift. It was the Bible from which my father had preached. The margins included many of his handwritten sermon notes. Just holding it in my hand, reading what my father thought about different passages of Scripture, was a sweet and tender experience for which I am deeply grateful.

But after my father had died, my mother had given that Bible to my abuser, because she so respected his godly heart.

In that moment, I didn't know what to do with the Bible. Treasure it? Or handle it with horror because it had belonged for a while to a man who led a double life?

I accepted the gift with gratitude, but I was later reminded again of the history of this Bible when I found some notes, sermon quotes, and tracts that I knew were not my father's because of the penmanship and the dates. They had been written in my father's Bible by the person who harmed me. Even in the middle of joy, we may find an unexpected reminder of evil.

"Will You Trust Me?"

Though we can never truly know the heart of another person, there is significant evidence to support the possibility that the person who harmed me was a believer. From the distance of many years, I can even imagine that there may have been in his heart a process of repentance and restoration. *I am in no way excusing what he did!* But once again, I am led to a place where God asks, "Will you trust me? Will you trust that when redemption is finally complete, all things will be made new?"

I have had tastes of wanting to see this person again at a time when both he and I would be changed and redemption in our hearts completed. Though we may not have certainty about others, we can still look forward to a day when our own hearts will be free of entanglements and sin and able to worship God with great joy. And we can long for God to reshape our hearts to desire this same redemption for others.

A Realization and a Calling

There is an outcome to my story for which I am deeply grateful. I was in my mid-thirties when I began to piece together the story of what had happened to me. I was in a seminar listening to Dan Allender speak about our wounded hearts. (It was even before Dan published his book, *The Wounded Heart.*) My memory of that moment is still crystal clear. I remember realizing without question that what had happened to me was sexual abuse. It was a stunning realization that left me both breathless and tearful. But so many hidden things began to make sense in my mind as I put the pieces of my life together in a new way.

The following day, as Dan talked more about what healing might look like, I had one of the clearest experiences of God's voice that I have ever had. I simply began to understand two things clearly. First was the reality that I am a victim of sexual abuse, but second, God was calling me to work with women and men who had been abused.

I left the conference and went home to tell my husband, Stuart, those two things. "I have been sexually abused. And God has called me to work in this field." He graciously accepted both statements with incredible love and support. And then we made a plan. I would enter counseling to work on the impact of my abuse and I would also return to school to pursue a graduate degree in counseling. There have been very few moments in my life when what I should do was as clear as this was. But it was a breath of fresh air to realize that there was hope and that God's calling would enable me to bring hope to others. To this day I am deeply thankful for both of those things.

I did enter counseling and came to know more about my story and the ways in which I had been damaged. But I also learned so much more about God's redeeming grace. I returned to school, graduated with a master's degree, and have worked more than twenty-five years as a counselor. I believe our stories are meant to be pictures of God's redemption even before they resolve, even before we understand all the details. You may remember the phrase from *The Lion, the Witch and the Wardrobe,* "Aslan is on the move." He is on the move in each of our lives and the good news of the gospel gives us the courage to look for his footprints even in difficult places. The goal is not to minimize the harm or to sugarcoat the sin. The goal is to look for trickles of grace, trickles of living water in a dry, thirsty land.

The Source of Forgiveness

God calls us to forgive and he makes us forgiving people. But it is rarely easy. God calls us to forgive and enables us to forgive, but he will always, again and again, bring us to places where we are completely and utterly dependent on him. He wants us to know him, to receive from him, to trust him, to understand that he is the only source of life we have!

And so, forgiveness is often not a one-time experience, but a lifelong process. Forgiveness calls us to trust the One who created us and loves us and has offered his forgiveness to us.

God has given us a fountain where we can drink again and again. But we sometimes refuse. Jeremiah 2:13 says, "My people have committed two evils: they have forsaken me, the fountain of living waters, and hewed out cisterns for themselves, broken cisterns that can hold no water."

Why are we afraid to drink? Here is God's promise: "The LORD will guide you continually and satisfy your desire in scorched places and make your bones strong; and you shall be like a watered garden, like a spring of water, whose waters do not fail" (Isaiah 58:11).

Would you rather be a broken cistern or a spring whose waters do not fail? Sometimes we refuse to drink because it seems dangerous.

- What if trusting God doesn't remove our pain and suffering?
- What if trusting God means we have to deal with sorrow that we don't understand?

God does not promise to deliver us out of the brokenness of the world, but he does offer to be our comfort and our peace in the struggle and the mess. We are often afraid of weakness, terrified of not having it all together. There is a powerlessness in receiving, standing before God, standing at the cross, and again realizing that we are empty-handed before the God of the universe.

Perhaps you know this hymn:

Nothing in my hands I bring,
Simply to thy cross I cling;

Naked, come to thee for dress,
Helpless, look to thee for grace;
Foul, I to the fountain fly;
Wash me, Savior, or I die.[1]

As we make our way through the process of forgiveness, we may feel as though we are naked and helpless. But we don't have to fear. The power of the Spirit is the power that raised Jesus from the dead. It can bring cold, dark, dead hearts to life. It can change us from persons who won't even acknowledge they are thirsty to those who drink so deeply that they can offer cold water to others who thirst.

Remember, forgiveness does not originate with us. It starts with being forgiven by God, and God invites each of us who are thirsty to come to the well of his incredible forgiveness. So come, drink, live, and find your heart willing to offer others the sweet water of forgiveness that has been offered to you.

Questions for Reflection

These questions are meant to help you think about something in your story that seems not quite right. There are no wrong answers and there is no need to delve deeply into your memories if something does not come quickly to your mind. The goal is simply to give you an opportunity to think through an event in your life that may need to be forgiven. If you are just beginning to think through a part of your story that involves some type of trauma, it may be helpful to answer these questions in the presence of a trusted friend or counselor.

1. Do you have a personal story of harm or loss? Think in terms of someone you trusted or depended on who treated you harshly, or with meanness, or who avoided you altogether. We all have times when we were shamed or spoken to in anger, or when we had to deal with

physical aggression, perhaps even from someone we didn't know. Your story may be a brief memory of a schoolyard bully or a story long enough to fill a book. It may be a simple story where a sibling destroys something you loved, a friend betrayed your trust, or a parent was unavailable when you needed him. Harm is not only what has been done to us. It can be something that was threatened or something that might have been missing in your life. Take a few moments to write something you remember about a story in your life.

2. How old were you when the event occurred?
3. Was there a betrayal of trust, however small, in the story?
4. Was something done to you, or was something important left undone?
5. Have you always remembered this story? When did you begin to remember it?
6. Does your story bring to mind someone you need to forgive? It may be helpful to keep this story in mind as you continue to read the book.

CHAPTER 5

Forgiveness and Anger

Kevin and Anna are a young married couple with three children. Kevin is the family pastor at a large church. Kevin and Anna's life revolves around the church since most of their friends attend there. They are also part of a homeschool group that includes other church families. While the senior pastor has always seemed supportive of Kevin, something seems to have changed and Kevin doesn't know why. Then a member of the church board told Kevin that there had been a meeting to evaluate Kevin's job performance. The senior pastor wanted to fire him. Apparently he had offended a high-profile family in the church with the way he handled a discipline incident with their child. Though Kevin had followed all of the church guidelines, the family was still angry that their child had been corrected.

Kevin tried to talk with his senior pastor but the pastor refused to discuss the problem with him. Anna was devastated by this news. She doesn't know who to trust among her friends and homeschool community. Neither Kevin nor Anna knows what to do next. Kevin says he is "disappointed." Anna says she is "just numb." If you asked them if they are angry, both would say they are not.

≈ ≈ ≈

One of the costs of forgiveness may involve facing our own anger, something that can be very hard to do. It is clearly possible for our anger to be motivated by a variety of thoughts and emotions. However, it should not be dismissed as an emotion to avoid. The Old Testament refers to "the anger of the Lord" nearly one hundred times so, while we are unable to be angry in the righteous way that God is angry, we are given examples of the things that anger him.

Sin in its many forms is the focus of God's ire. David in Psalm 6:1 begs God not to be angry with him, and in Psalm 7:6 he pleads with God to be angry with David's enemies. God's anger at evil is just and righteous.

Because God's wrath was poured out on Jesus on the cross where he paid the price for our sin, the wrath of God is no longer something we need to fear. Paul writes of this good news in Romans 5:9: "Since, therefore, we have now been justified by his blood, much more shall we be saved by him from the wrath of God." And we are reminded again in 1 Thessalonians 5:9 that, as believers, "God has not destined us for wrath, but to obtain salvation through our Lord Jesus Christ."

Since we know these things, the truth that God continues to be angered by evil can help us when we have angry feelings over evil done to us or to others. There is a kind of righteous anger that refuses to call evil good.

Diane Langberg, Ph.D., a Christian therapist known for her work with trauma victims around the world, wrote about it in *Suffering and the Heart of God: How Trauma Destroys and Christ Restores*. In an interview she said,

> "As Christians, we are called to righteousness. You cannot have righteousness without truth. . . . Righteousness declares the truth—not just about good things but also about evil, sin and suffering. Sometimes the most righteous thing is the facts about evil; facts that need to be named and

to which we are called to respond. To pretend that an affair or pornography or hatred of others is a little thing is to deceive ourselves and others. Deception is what the enemy does . . . . It is, therefore, unrighteous. Also, in reducing evil to little or nothing we fail to see the work of Christ on the cross in truth. There is *no* evil he has not borne."[1]

Langberg is reminding us that our fear of naming evil, of being angry over evil's impact, or perhaps of tapping into the anger of others is no excuse for pretending that evil does not exist. To do so, Langberg notes, is to minimize the reality of the cross where Jesus took on every bit of evil. Evil must be called exactly what it is, and that may well involve godly anger.

In some ways, anger is a very natural response to pain. Think about stubbing your toe or banging your elbow. It hurts—a lot—and isn't it true that your internal response is often anger? Pain can lead to angry contempt turned either toward ourselves for being so foolish as to stub our toe, or toward someone else who inadvertently tripped us or left something lying in our path.

To avoid anger, we might attempt to "take the hit" when it comes to the pain by embracing denial that says, "I've actually not been hurt at all." This is not a good long-term solution, because unexpressed anger will always find a way to express itself in some way, be it physically, emotionally, or spiritually (or in all three ways).

The Problem with Anger

We may find it difficult to confront our own angry heart. Certainly Kevin and Anna are finding it hard. A heart filled with anger, our own or someone else's, can be hard to face. We may be afraid our anger will be out of control, so it feels dangerous to admit that we are angry. We often find that anger leads us to sin ourselves. Even worse, if I am angry, I am fearful that I am like the one who harmed me.

The truth is that when a person sins against us, anger is often part of our response. Paul tells us in Ephesians 4:26, "Be angry and do not sin." The NIV makes it a little clearer, saying, "In your anger do not sin," and the NLT clears it up to say, "Don't sin by letting anger control you."

From this verse we can see that anger is a powerful emotion that God calls us to use wisely. We need to consider Paul's caution and the ways we might be controlled by our anger. Remember, it is not only when anger erupts in loud words and angry gestures that we are controlled by it. Anger also controls us when our hearts become hard and cold, filled with animosity and bitterness. Silence or physical separation can express anger in a way that makes it harder for others to know how to respond. Sometimes persons who are frequently angry have learned how to make subtle, confusing shifts from anger to silence. Suddenly it appears as if the other person in the conversation is the angry one, while the genuinely angry person appears quite peaceful. This controls and confuses the person who might otherwise confront the angry person about his attitudes and behavior.

If we find ourselves afraid to be angry, or we refuse to be angry, we may feel pulled into denial and untruthfulness. The result can leave us numb and flat, where almost all emotion is restrained. In that place, with our hearts safely numbed, we can continue to deny that there is anything to be angry about; we can say that we certainly are not feeling that "wrong" emotion. But saying that we are not angry doesn't make it the truth. Something may still be wrong and we may still be angry about it.

Using Anger Wisely

Think about what Kevin and Anna are facing. They have experienced genuine hurt. They are angry (although neither can quite say that). Instead of venting their anger so that it leads to sin or denying their anger so that they are cut off from reality, how might they wisely use the anger that accompanies pain or loss?

Their anger is justified. They have been treated badly. Our anger may also be justified. When we are angry about the things that anger God, we reflect his image. But, unlike God, we are incapable of automatically using our anger in a way that reflects his glory.

Paul reminds us in Ephesians 4:31-32 that we are to "let all bitterness and wrath and anger and clamor and slander be put away from you, along with all malice. Be kind to one another, tenderhearted, forgiving one another, as God in Christ forgave you."

This is no easy task. None of us has a toggle switch that takes us from bitterness to kindness or from rage to forgiveness. Paul is encouraging a process, and a difficult one at that, which is why we often go to great lengths to avoid it.

Acknowledging the truth of our hearts is the beginning of change. For Kevin and Anna and for you and me, putting words to that reality is the first step. But when hatred, rage, and murderous thoughts take up residence in our hearts, they quickly set up a battleground. Guilty and ashamed, we find it hard to talk with God about the reality that is driving our lives.

We need not fear this part of the journey. Prayer invites us toward honesty and perhaps into the very process of describing our anger. Writing or drawing may be other ways to describe this strong emotion. Can you describe how you feel when you are angry about a wrong done to you? If you are unsure, a friend, a spouse, or a child might be able to tell you what you are like when you are angry or even help you to put words to what you feel. Kevin and Anna took the first step in this process when they acknowledged to each other how hurt and angry they felt. There . . . the truth was out! Now they could start to pray with and for each other about how to be angry and not sin. It was the beginning of a long journey.

How Facing Anger Can Strengthen Faith

On that journey, Kevin, Anna, you, and I have been given many models of how to bring our anger and hurt to God in prayer. Many of the psalms are personal journals of the writer's struggle with anger and confusion about evils the psalmist has seen and experienced. For instance, in Psalm 73:3, 5, Asaph describes his envy of the wicked because they seem to live without problems. He says, "For I was envious of the arrogant when I saw the prosperity of the wicked. . . . They are not in trouble as others are; they are not stricken like the rest of mankind." But Asaph, a worship leader in Israel, goes on to say that it was in God's sanctuary that he began to understand. He tells God, "Truly you set them in slippery places; you make them fall to ruin" (v. 18). They are, as Asaph describes, "swept away utterly by terrors" (v. 19). He ends this worshipful psalm reflectively: "When my soul was embittered . . . I was like a beast toward you [God]" (vv. 21–22). God's compassion and invitation stand in strong contrast to the place where Asaph's fears had taken him. In verses 23 and 24 Asaph writes, "Nevertheless, I am continually with you; you hold my right hand. You guide me with your counsel, and afterward you will receive me to glory." In verses 27 and 28 he closes his worship with these words: "For behold, those who are far from you shall perish; you put an end to everyone who is unfaithful to you. But for me it is good to be near God; I have made the LORD God my refuge, that I may tell of all your works."

Dan Allender reminds us in his book, *The Cry of the Soul*, that "righteous anger is willing to struggle and wait."[2] Most of us are not fond of either struggling or waiting. But righteous anger does grieve and struggle with God, asking the same kinds of questions as Asaph did:

"What are you doing, God?"

"What am I to understand about you?"

"What do I need to face about myself, given the fury that I feel?"

"Do you know that my heart is broken?"

"When will this end?"

These are some of the things we might express as we wait and struggle. Do any of them sound familiar to you?

Honestly describing our angry hearts to God does not have to be an exercise in venting our rage. It is, as Allender said, a place of "struggle" and a place of "waiting." And in that place we may need to face hard realities about our hearts that are similar to Asaph's experience. We may rant and rave, we may find hatred joining the chorus, we may be angry at everyone including God, or place our anger on those around us. But something crucial, though perhaps unexpected, may happen in this process. As we listen to our own thoughts and words, we may find that we can no longer describe ourselves as faultless.

We find it extremely difficult to be angry without sin, especially when we have been deeply harmed. And as we begin to see our own need for forgiveness from God and perhaps from others, the gap between our foe and us may seem a bit less. Gradually, the one who harmed us seems less "alien" and different. We may even begin to understand how, in some ways, we are like the one who harmed us. This realization encourages us to go to our Great High Priest, described for us in Hebrews 4:14–16, where God tells us that he has given us an amazing Intercessor who understands our weakness though he was without sin. Jesus will offer us mercy and help when we need it.

> Since then we have a great high priest who has passed through the heavens, Jesus, the Son of God, let us hold fast our confession. For we do not have a high priest who is unable to sympathize with our weaknesses, but one who in every respect has been tempted as we are, yet without sin. Let us then with confidence draw near to the throne of grace, that we may receive mercy and find grace to help in time of need.

What is your weakness when it comes to anger? How can you ask your Great High Priest to help you in your time of need? Certainly Kevin and Anna felt their weakness keenly as they struggled with anger and hurt. There was no quick fix for their difficult work situation or their broken relationships. But as they honestly poured their hearts to God and to each other, the Spirit did help them. Gradually they began to get a vision of how to move forward in a difficult situation. The same High Priest who helped Kevin and Anna can and will help you if you ask, and this will strengthen you to learn what you need to learn from the following chapters.

Questions for Reflection

1. How might the different ways of managing anger keep your heart from moving toward forgiveness? Compare your normal anger responses with your response when you are moving through the process of forgiveness.

2. If you are afraid to be angry, what is the result of your fear?

3. How do you think others close to you might describe their experience of you when there is a reason to be angry, but you refuse to acknowledge your anger?

4. What does your display of anger look like in public? With family and friends? When you are alone?

5. What kind of language do you use to express your anger? (Remember that silence can be an icy way to express your anger.) Is your anger language the same in private as it is in public?

6. Think of a time when you were furious at someone who hurt you. What was going on in your heart then (or perhaps even now)?

7. If you struggle with anger, how can the words from Hebrews give you confidence that you can come to God in weakness?

CHAPTER 6

Renouncing Revenge

Doug worked for a small computer company where he had a few good friends, including Jim. He and Jim often hung out together after work and sometimes enjoyed biking with other friends on weekends. They talked a lot about their jobs and discovered that they both felt overlooked and overworked by their boss. One Monday morning they were called to a meeting with some of the top executives in their company, where they learned that they were both being considered for a promotion. Doug and Jim were each asked to share a strength and a weakness. When it was Jim's turn, Doug was stunned to hear Jim say, "Well, I think I might be a better fit for this job since there are times when Doug complains about his assignments."

Doug left the meeting stunned and furious. Soon his mind turned to ways he could get back at Jim. Scheme after scheme ran through his mind, including things he could say about Jim's work ethic to their boss, or ways he could rehash for their boss all the complaints and criticisms that Jim had made about him during many conversations. Doug thought about going to the boss to tell him these things. He definitely planned on warning his coworkers to be careful around Jim because he was so untrustworthy. He kept thinking of how foolish he had been to trust Jim and how he would never trust anyone again. Planning how to get back at Jim didn't mask the rage and pain he felt from being betrayed by his friend. But Doug still desperately wanted to get even.

≈ ≈ ≈

Never avenge yourselves, but leave it to the wrath of God, for it is written, "Vengeance is mine, I will repay, says the Lord." (Romans 12:19)

What Doug wanted to do in response to Jim's betrayal is described by Paul as trying to "avenge" ourselves. That simply means getting back at someone who has hurt us. When I hear the word *avenge*, my thoughts go something like this: "Oh, I'm not a vengeful person. I just let things go. I wouldn't take revenge."

And then I think of the elaborate mental schemes I can concoct when someone cuts in front of me in the checkout line at the grocery store. I sometimes ponder for hours what I should have said or what the person needs to hear.

How about you? Can you relate to Doug and his desire to get back at Jim? Or to me in the checkout line? Think about your responses to the following situations:

- How do you respond when someone deliberately cuts you off in traffic after you have patiently waited to pull out?
- After working for weeks on a project at work, how did your heart respond when your boss failed to acknowledge your hard work to your team but acted as though he had produced the document himself?
- You were having a conversation with a friend, who completely misunderstood what you were saying and accused you of the very thing you had carefully avoided.

- You always know where your keys are because you have a specific place to put them as you come into the house. Your roommate wants to borrow your car and you generously agree, but you cannot find your keys. What happens when she casually mentions, "Oh, you never know where your keys are"?
- You worked long and hard to develop a new plan for small group ministry in your church. You arrive at a staff meeting, excited to share it. Instead, you hear the lead pastor say, "We were planning to launch a new plan for small groups, but we have decided that the greater need is training for our elders." That is all the explanation you receive.

None of these examples involve life-damaging experiences. They fall more into the everyday irritant category. But that is just the point. We may think that we are not vengeful, but when we are dismissed, when we experience something unfair, when we have offered something good and receive the opposite in return, we may find ourselves quickly responding, either out loud or in our mind, with words that are critical, denigrating, and sometimes hanging on the edge of violence.

What moves us toward these thoughts and sometimes even these behaviors? A number of researchers say that revenge stimulates a part of our brain that makes us feel good and experience temporary satisfaction.[1] We have all heard the saying, "Revenge is sweet," and it may feel so in the moment, but the consequences to actually carrying out revenge are not sweet at all. They are sour, harmful, and very difficult to undo. That is why God provides a rescue that will not cause more harm.

Paul reminds us that we don't have to respond to harm with behaviors that damage us or others. He says that revenge belongs to God, and God will be in charge of the outcome. I have just recently begun to understand that renouncing revenge and allowing God to be the sentencing judge is not just because he is better at finding the truth and knowing what needs to be done. It is also because he is saving us from harm. There is harm in revenge—*perhaps* to the offender. We may be able to carry that out in some way. But we need to remember that when we pursue vengeance, even in our imagination, there is a price we pay as well. The process will definitely impact our hearts and could even damage our health.

Powerful or Powerless?

God certainly seems capable of keeping things under control in this arena, so what makes it hard for us to renounce revenge? Isn't it because the thought of getting back at someone makes us feel powerful? How many hours can you spend rehearsing a conversation in which you felt slighted or challenged or where anger was expressed at you? We can work things like that over and over in our heads (or with someone else) until we think of exactly the right response to "get" the other person. Someone has "stuck it to us" and we can't stop thinking about how we could have come back at them.

A short time ago, a friend told me about a career situation where someone rendered her powerless, accused her, and shamed her. My response? I not only tried to come up with a really good comeback while we were talking, I have been thinking about it ever since. And it didn't even happen to me!

To be betrayed with information shared in friendship so that someone can gain an advantage in the workplace is a painful experience. Just ask Doug. However, although angry thoughts of revenge may numb the pain Doug feels in the moment, the outcome of revenge eventually harms the person who was betrayed at least as much (and perhaps more) than the one who betrayed the friendship.

Our hearts leap at the chance of getting back at someone, but God says that vengeance belongs to him. While we may believe that to be true, we often think that there is no harm in dreaming and scheming about what vengeance might look like, or how good it would feel to us and how devastating it could be to the one who harmed us.

But there *is* harm in concocting scenarios of revenge. It seems to let off steam in the moment, but when our desire is to gain the upper hand and "get even," there is a physical as well as emotional and spiritual price to pay. Physically, anger can impact our bodies, but when we take things into our own hands, as though God cannot be trusted to deal with the one who harmed us, there is a high emotional and spiritual cost. We walk away from the One who can protect us and help us to work through a healthier response to what has harmed us.

The Cost of Revenge

The Bible teaches us that revenge is costly—to the person who takes God's place and tries to get even! In Isaiah 30, God is pursuing his people but they won't listen. It begins with these words: "'Ah, stubborn children,' declares the LORD, 'who carry out a plan, but not mine, and who make an alliance, but not of my Spirit, that they may add sin to sin.'" God goes on to describe how the Israelites pursued other options and refused to listen when God through his prophets called them back to himself. Listen to the way God pursued them in verses 15–17:

> For thus said the Lord GOD, the Holy One of Israel,
> "In returning and rest you shall be saved; in quietness and in trust shall be your strength." But you were unwilling, and you said, "No! We will flee upon horses"; therefore you shall flee away; and, "We will ride upon swift steeds"; therefore your pursuers shall be swift. A thousand shall flee at the threat of one; at the threat of five you shall flee till you are left like a flagstaff on the top of a mountain, like a signal on a hill."

This is a fine description of where revenge can take us. When we take revenge, we believe that our own acumen and strength will save us. It is very similar to Israel riding on "swift steeds." But our outcome is also similar. We will be pursued until there is no place to go and we will be as exposed as a flag on the top of a mountain.

Revenge exposes us to all kinds of risks and dangers. We may succeed in carrying out a detailed plan of revenge where we see the offender suffer, but we will pay a severe price ourselves. When we plot revenge, we redirect our brains into problem- solving mode. However, this is not a math problem or a plot in a well-written novel; this is a scheme that focuses for hours and hours on harming someone we know. It involves real anger and an intense focus on inflicting harm, real or imagined. Revenge threatens to take charge of us more and more by occupying our every thought with negativity. The result is damage to our hearts, our bodies, our friends, and our families. The self-centered focus of revenge is almost always evident to those around us. And it is destructive to relationships, to our health, and certainly to our faith. In the end, the impact is worse for us than for anyone else, and the recovery process can be long and difficult. When we choose independence instead of leaving revenge to God, we end up, says Isaiah, out in the open like a flag on a hilltop.

Plotting vengeance will also cause us to miss something else God promises in this Isaiah passage: "Therefore the LORD waits to be gracious to you, and therefore he exalts himself to show mercy to you. *For the LORD is a God of justice; blessed are all those who wait for him*" (v. 18, emphasis mine).

When we are willing to renounce revenge and turn our heart to God, he promises rest, trust, strength, and eventual justice.

Justice vs. Vengeance

Renouncing revenge doesn't mean that we have to renounce justice. There may be situations when we renounce revenge only to realize that justice needs to be pursued. Certainly, in the process of forgiveness, there may be things that are appropriate to overlook, but our desire for justice may not be the thing to put aside. In fact, the Isaiah 30 passage reminds us that "the LORD is a God of justice." When there has been great harm or loss, pursuing justice may be an important part of our response.

Jesus rebuked the Pharisees for neglecting justice (Matthew 23:23), and there are times when God may call us to actively pursue justice. There are evil actions that require this pursuit. But justice and vengeance are not the same. Seeking justice with a heart that knows its own sin, lives in ongoing repentance, and desires to forgive bears no resemblance to pursuing revenge. And if we refuse to seek justice in a way that calls someone away from sin, it may be that we are still holding on to revenge. It's as if we were saying, "I will not do anything good toward these people. I refuse to care what happens to them. They made their bed, let them lie in it."

It can seem difficult to heed God's call to repentance and rest while we pursue justice. But that is exactly the heart attitude we want when we are in a situation where justice is important. We need to be repentant for our own sin and we need to long for the one who harmed us to also have a change of heart. We look at our own hearts, we repent of what we know to be sin, and we rest in God as we grow in our understanding of how justice may bring the one who harmed us back from the brink.

But how do we relinquish our "right" to revenge? How could we possibly be willing to offer *any* good, even in the form of justice, to someone who has caused so much harm?

Entrusting Ourselves to God

For to this you have been called, because Christ also suffered for you, leaving you an example, so that you might follow in his steps. He committed no sin, neither was deceit found in his mouth. When he was reviled, he did not revile in return; when he suffered, he did not threaten, but continued entrusting himself to him who judges justly. (1 Peter 2:21–23)

We have to begin this process by doing what Jesus did. We commit our cause to the One who judges justly. Jesus "entrusted" himself to God for justice. What we see in Jesus is a willingness to trust the Father. It did not mean that he would be spared shame or even physical suffering. Jesus was harmed without cause, as you may have been. But in that place of abuse, his heart was able to release the offenders—even from the cross—and to rest, though the price was high and the pain was great.

Jesus knew what we would need to remember—that God would deal with his abusers and ours. Jesus knew and remembered the end of the story, and we can too. God gives us hope that one day everything will be made right.

Perhaps you recall that great scene in J. R. R. Tolkien's *The Return of the King,* when Gandalf is reunited with Frodo and Sam. Sam is so surprised to see Gandalf that he says, "I thought you were dead. But then I thought I was dead . . . What is happening?" Gandalf responds, ". . . the land is in the keeping of the King. A great shadow is gone." And then Sam asks him this poignant question: "Is everything sad going to come untrue?"[2]

This is such a picture of hope! Hope that one day there will be ultimate justice, based on the outcome of Christ's death on the cross. The writer reminds us in Hebrews 10:23, "Let us hold fast the confession of our hope without wavering, for he who promised is faithful." What will it be like on that day?

In Revelation, John tells us, "Behold, the dwelling place of God is with man. He will dwell with them, and they will be his people, and God himself will be with them as their God. He will wipe away every tear from their eyes, and death shall be no more, neither shall there be mourning, nor crying, nor pain anymore, for the former things have passed away" (Revelation 21:3–4).

When we entrust ourselves to the just Judge, what happens to those we release to God? Either they will repent and Jesus will take their punishment, or they will harden their hearts and God will eventually be their judge, without the sacrifice of Christ to cover their sin.

Surrender and Trust

It is hard for us to let go of our false sense of control over the process, yet God calls us to surrender our need for revenge to him and to rest . . . as Jesus did. This is the first part of what God is calling Doug to do in response to Jim's betrayal. Doug needs to entrust himself to God. He has to remember that nothing can separate him from God's love, not even Jim's betrayal. He needs to trust and rest in God's love for him.

Doug, you, and I are not the only ones who have struggled with this. Many writers of the Psalms ask God about the wicked who seem to go unpunished. Earlier, we looked at Psalm 73, written by Asaph, a choir director, as he wrestled with this question. In Psalm 77 he again cries out to God from a place where his "soul refuses to be comforted" (v. 2). He goes on to describe his moaning, his fainting spirit. How does he escape from this dark place? He says, "I will remember the deeds of the LORD . . . I will ponder all your work" (vv. 11–12). For the rest of the psalm, he remembers what God has done. He talks about God's power in creation. But the last verses are some of my favorites. Asaph says, "Your way was through the sea, your path through the great waters; yet your footprints were unseen. You led your people like a flock by the hand of Moses and Aaron."

These verses describe a place in which we often find ourselves. Asaph is remembering how the Israelites left Egypt, but there are often "seas" in my life where it seems I will surely drown. Yet Asaph says that though God's way was through the sea, his "footprints" were unseen and his people were led by the hand. Whose hand? The hands of Moses and Aaron.

They were, as we often are, asked to walk through something when they could not see God, his plan, or the path. But he does have a plan. And in this case he used Aaron and Moses as his representatives. The people followed them as if they were following God.

If you are struggling through a difficult time, especially in terms of forgiveness, and you feel like there is no path and no hand held out to you, remember that God's hand is sometimes offered through those who love and trust him. Don't feel as though you must tough it out on your own. Find people you can trust and take them into your confidence. Ask them to pray with you and for you. Ask if they can see a path that you cannot discern. And remember that God is our ultimate Rescuer and his promises are true to the very end.

> This is my Father's world,
> O let me ne'er forget
> That though the wrong seems oft so strong,
> God is the Ruler yet.[3]

First Peter 3:8–9 reads, "Finally, all of you, have unity of mind, sympathy, brotherly love, a tender heart, and a humble mind. Do not repay evil for evil or reviling for reviling, but on the contrary, bless, for to this you were called, that you may obtain a blessing." In 3:18, Peter reminds us, "For Christ also suffered once for sins, the righteous for the unrighteous, that he might being us to God."

We are not able to live like this without the power of the gospel. We are people who repay and revile others, even if we never act out our thoughts. But Jesus came to our rescue while we were (are) still unrighteous. He took the vengeance we deserved. Jesus was the object of the greatest revenge ever plotted, though he was not guilty of anything that deserved the rage he received. He paid the cost that was ours.

Questions for Reflection

1. Think about one time when you were tempted to seek revenge. Why? What was the result?
2. Can you think of a time when someone tried to get revenge on you? Why? What was the result?
3. In Ephesians 4:26, Paul tells us, "Be angry and do not sin." How can this verse help us when we are tempted to indulge in revenge, even in our thoughts?
4. Think about the following phrases from Isaiah 53:

   v. 4: "Surely he has borne our griefs and carried our sorrows."

   v. 5: "He was pierced for our transgressions; he was crushed for our iniquities."

   vv. 8, 9: "By oppression and judgment he was taken away; . . . they made his grave with the wicked . . . although he had done no violence."

   v. 10: "Yet it was the will of the LORD to crush him; he has put him to grief."

   v. 11: "Out of the anguish of his soul he shall see and be satisfied; . . . the righteous one, my servant [shall] make many to be accounted righteous, and he shall bear their iniquities."

   - What is your heart response to how Jesus suffered for us?
   - What words in the Isaiah passage are most helpful to you?
   - How may these reminders help you to renounce revenge?
   - How shall we then live, love, and respond to those who have sinned against us? How might these verses help you to continue on as Jesus did, "entrusting himself to him who judges justly"?

CHAPTER 7

How to Forgive Monsters and Other Normal Sinners

I was once asked to give a talk on forgiveness at a conference. I was even given the title: "How to Forgive Monsters and Other Normal Sinners." My first response was to think of the big blue hairy guy and the little green eyeball from *Monsters Inc.* But that wasn't what the conference organizer had in mind. The topic for the conference was the life of Joseph, and I had been asked to talk about what forgiveness looked like for him. Joseph's life reads like an epic saga. Though it begins in Genesis 30:24 when Joseph is born, the details stretch out from Genesis 35:24 to Genesis 50:26, where Joseph died in Egypt at the age of 110. And in the story of Joseph you see some of the complexity of forgiveness.

I liked the title of the talk since any of us may find ourselves needing to forgive people in both categories—"monsters" and "normal sinners." We are certainly all "normal" sinners who need to be forgiven every day. But there are also people in the world whose capacity for evil takes our breath away. You may, as I did, encounter them in your own neighborhood, your own family, or on the other side of the world.

Joseph's Encounters with Evil—and Good

Joseph had people like that in his life too. He began his life as the favored son of his father Jacob. His status was (unwisely) made abundantly clear by his father's special treatment. Joseph also had dreams in which his family (including his eleven brothers) bowed down to him, which he shared with apparent disregard for how his brothers would receive it. Eventually his resentful brothers captured him while they were all far from home, sold him to slave traders heading for Egypt, and told Jacob that Joseph had been killed by a wild animal. While Jacob mourned, Joseph endured betrayals and disappointments as a slave in Egypt. But eventually his God-given ability to interpret dreams brought him to a place of honor and power as Pharaoh's chief official. In that capacity he saved the nation from famine—and his own family as well.

Tim Keller once pointed out that there is an "asymmetrical relationship" between God and evil or suffering. Satan is never an equal with God, which helps us to remember that God is in absolute control. He may permit evil but he also limits it, even when we are unable to see those limits. Suffering may be the best place to learn to love God for himself alone, when we are willing to trust his character though we do not understand what he is doing. This may mean that we choose to live for God even without an answer to our questions.

God's Steadfast Love

We see this in Joseph's story. After his brothers betrayed him and he ended up in Egypt, Genesis 39:2 says, "The LORD was with Joseph, and he became a successful man." Even Joseph's employer Potiphar could see "that the LORD was with him and that the LORD caused all that he did to succeed in his hands. So Joseph found favor in his sight . . . and he made him overseer of his house and put him in charge of all that he had" (Genesis 39:3–4).

Have you ever wondered how, when, or where Joseph learned to trust God? His job in Potiphar's house was an outcome of the harm done to him by his brothers. He was in Egypt because he had been sold by his brothers to slave traders who sold him to Potiphar.

Then, as he continued in Potiphar's house, he chose to refuse the affection of Potiphar's wife and ran away from her. Again he was treated unfairly, betrayed, and discredited by the lies of Potiphar's wife. In anger, Potiphar put him in prison. It is incredibly difficult to choose to do the right thing and receive evil in return. The natural cry of our heart may easily be, "God, where are you?" In Joseph's story, we know God was there, because the text tells us, "The LORD was with Joseph and showed him steadfast love and gave him favor in the sight of the keeper of the prison" (Genesis 39:21).

What is your response when you are harmed, betrayed, and falsely accused? I want God to make it right and to punish those who are responsible. But God's path with Joseph was to grow Joseph in God's "steadfast love" (Genesis 39:21). What a tender movement on God's part. He not only engineered favor for Joseph but he was "with him" and helped him to see God's "steadfast love" as he was imprisoned.

In Genesis 45 Joseph reveals his identity to his brothers. He had already tested them in a number of ways. He is forthright in acknowledging the harm they had done to him. He never minimizes it, but he says, "And now do not be distressed or angry with yourselves because you sold me here, for God sent me before you to preserve life" (v. 5). Their intended evil had been used for good in Joseph's life and, even more astounding, in his brothers' lives. Joseph's presence and role in Egypt was a rescue for his family and many others.

Joseph sums it up in Genesis 50 when his brothers come to ask him for forgiveness after Jacob's death. He tells them,

"'Do not fear, for am I in the place of God? As for you, you meant evil against me but God meant it for good, to bring it about that many people should be kept alive, as they are today. So do not fear, I will provide for you and your little ones.' Thus he comforted them and spoke kindly to them." (vv. 19–21)

Surely God intends us to read this story and by faith believe that he can be trusted to bring good from evil. We do not always see how God deals with those who have harmed us. In fact, we may even see them prosper, but in this story God shows us that the long arm of evil is not beyond his reach. We are therefore never out of his hand of care and blessing.

Facing Evil with Faith

Joseph's statement is helpful as he testifies to the ways God used evil for good in his life and the lives of others. But it's also helpful in its straightforward acknowledgment that there are people who mean to do evil, in Joseph's world and in ours. We live in a world where evil will be encountered, and it may have a tremendous impact on our lives. Global terrorism may disrupt our safety, or a neighbor or even a family member may have evil intentions that leave their mark on us for a lifetime.

Some of these events involve evil at a level that can shake our moral foundations. They may be well-planned in advance or random acts of violence. Often we discover that they have been committed in what we thought was a safe place by someone we thought could be trusted. Seemingly unforgivable acts leave us with unanswered questions about God and about the nature of evil. But even in these places, God invites us to trust him. He is not a God we can control but he is a God who can be trusted. C. S. Lewis made this point so aptly in *The Lion, The Witch and the Wardrobe* when he wrote about Aslan, "Of course he isn't safe. But he's good. He's the King, I tell you."[1]

Understanding Evil

What is the source of the evil that prompts the heinous things that human beings do? What is the source of evil in our own hearts? We may not carry out all our evil intentions but we certainly think about them and often enjoy it. We'd like to think that source of the problem is as rare as the incidents themselves are extreme, but God's answer is simpler. Romans 1:25 talks about people who "exchanged the truth about God for a lie and worshiped and served the creature rather than the Creator." This must ring true for us because we often worship and serve ourselves rather than God.

Here Paul is identifying the root of evil: people worship themselves instead of God. Sometimes they think they *are* God as they make choices to serve themselves in defiance of God's command. Even as I write this, I think you may agree that it is not "they" who do this. *We* do this.

It began in Genesis 3, when Eve ate the forbidden fruit in rebellion against God because the serpent told her it would make her "like God, knowing good and evil." Bible scholar Derek Kidner says that Eve was given "an opportunity to be self-made, wresting one's knowledge, satisfactions, and values from the created world in defiance of the Creator."[2] The Tree of Knowledge offered Adam and Eve an alternative to dependence on God. So the nature of evil is rebellion against God and setting ourselves up as God.

Is there any evil where rebellion against God is *not* the core issue? I think not, because the underlying issue in all of God's law has to do with God's honor and character being violated by my selfish choice. The commandments against murder, adultery, stealing, coveting, and lying are all about a refusal to trust God and taking things into my own hands.

Once Adam and Eve disobeyed God, their knowledge of good and evil became a personal experience in their souls. Evil was no longer an abstract concept. And this sinful nature was passed down to all of us.

Is Anything Truly Unforgivable?

So are we all evil in the sense that we attempt to be independent of God, choosing instead to go our own way? The answer is Yes. "All we like sheep have gone astray; we have turned—every one—to his own way," Isaiah 53:6 tells us. It adds, "and the LORD has laid on him [Jesus] the iniquity of us all." God's pardon is offered to "all who have sinned" and trust in Christ. That is why we need to come to terms with God's declaration that there is nothing that is actually "unforgivable" for the person who repents and trusts in Christ.

Scripture talks about things that seem unforgivable, but the door to redemption always remains open. In 1 Corinthians 6:6–11, when Paul lists specific sins that will exclude people from the kingdom of God, he ends by saying, "And such were some of you. But you were washed, you were sanctified, you were justified in the name of the Lord Jesus Christ and by the Spirit of our God." That is God's answer.

This is an important point, but often a difficult one for those who have experienced harm that seems unforgivable. Even if that hasn't been our experience, most of us are much more comfortable describing evil as something "out there" than we are in identifying it within our own hearts.

In a strange way, we are both terrified of and curious about evil. When the news reports that a father murdered his daughter, our hearts respond with questions like, "How can that be possible? Who could do such a thing?" And when the press releases a photograph of a normal-looking man, we want to know, "What went wrong? What happened to him? Is this person less than human or is he more like me than I want to recognize?"

Clearly, some things are far more difficult to forgive than others. But if we declare someone beyond forgiveness, we too have gone our own way to make god-like judgments that God has not made.

If we say that something is unforgivable, we risk damage to our own hearts because we are living independently of God. And we are also blind to the potential for sin that the Bible says exists within our own hearts.

The Danger of Self-Deceit and Denial

Very ordinary people sometimes do extraordinary evil. The genocide in Rwanda included torture, rape, and murder, not only by leaders and soldiers, but by neighbors—to those living next door, to those they had lived with peacefully for years. Something changed in the way they saw their neighbors and the way they saw themselves, and they refused to confront it.

Self-deceit is a significant part of a person's descent into evil. When we refuse to know the truth about ourselves because we want to avoid facing evil, we begin to hide. Self-deception is common but it can lead us to desperate places because it keeps us from acknowledging truth.

In April, 1945, the 89th Infantry Division liberated the concentration camp at Ohrdruf, Germany. American soldiers wrote vivid descriptions of the nightmarish conditions they found in the camp. Part of the horror of the place was the stench and the remains of many bodies incinerated there. The local townspeople, however, denied any knowledge of its existence. The mayor claimed he did not know of the camp's existence, though he committed suicide after its liberation.

We may deny the reality of evil because we are afraid to pay the cost of becoming involved or because we are unsure of what to do. In the case of Ohrdruf, an entire town of people responded, "We just didn't know." But that denial made them complicit in the evil that was done, no matter what they said.

Perhaps you can think of an example of how denial has kept you from confronting evil or wrongdoing. Your example could range from ignoring a relative's alcohol problem to refusing to confront the mean-spirited gossip of a friend. Regardless, God calls you to something different—and better.

Confronting Evil as We Forgive

Ignoring evil and living in denial are not options for believers who are called to forgive as they have been forgiven. Forgiveness does not shrink from the horror of evil. It actually confronts horror. When we forgive, we face that horror full on. We do not minimize, excuse, or tolerate it. Lewis Smedes, in his book *Forgive and Forget* says,

> To be able to forgive we must have the guts to look hard at the wrongness, the horridness, the sheer wickedness of what somebody did to us . . . One prime reason why some people cannot forgive is their fear of reality . . . Self-deception is a lot easier than forgiving. Forgiving begins with the power to shake off deception and deal with reality.[3]

We can be certain that God will exercise ultimate justice against evil. But in the meantime, our efforts to forgive evil lead us to acknowledge the existence of evil in our own hearts. Because of the gospel, we can avoid the descent into the self-deception that denies our own sinfulness. We can face the reality of who we are. Christ has dealt with the things we want to cover up. Since he has covered them with his righteousness, I am free to recognize my own evil heart. This also helps me to understand how evil functions in the hearts of others.

For example, I am not a serial killer, but I understand some of the dynamics of power, control, lust, and murder. Even though the gospel has brought enormous change to my heart, I still sin.

I have sin patterns that have existed for years and they are often still apparent. The change I desire does not come from denying my sin but from acknowledging it.

Think of a sin pattern in your life. It may be a significant addiction, a quick temper, or a critical, self-righteous spirit. What effect does it have on you, your friends, your family, your job, or your health? How might this pattern worsen if you deny its seriousness and impact?

Forgiveness—even forgiving what seems unforgivable—does not mean there is an absence of consequences or a refusal to pursue justice. When we renounce revenge, we commit our cause to God who judges justly. When we are free from a desire for vengeance, we may need to pursue justice as a way of loving the offender. There may be a penalty for the offender; however, whatever cost the offender pays will not be enough to cover the debt. Only Jesus can do that, as he took upon himself the pain and debt of our sin against him. The result is our salvation, a right relationship with God through Christ. Whether or not the perpetrator accepts God's grace, the payment Jesus made for sin still exists. This is the "now" of God's provision and we can rest in that. The "not yet" is a future day when we will witness the final destruction of evil. The Bible is graphic in its description of the eventual end of the wicked, detailing even our participation in the final demise of evil. Paul writes in Romans 16:20, "The God of peace will soon crush Satan under your feet."

We can rest in this promise.

A Story of Forgiveness

I want to tell you a true story (used with permission) about a woman who took these lessons to heart. It enabled her to confront and forgive evil in a remarkable and powerful way.

Sarah (her name has been changed) grew up in a close-knit farming community.

Her family was well known there and her parents were active in the church that they regularly attended.

Her father was an angry and abusive man. There was a great deal of physical violence within the family. Almost all problems were solved with painful physical punishment for each family member, including the mother. Sarah and her sister learned quickly to hide and to stay as far away as possible from her father's rage.

But in spite of their caution, from the time she was a young child, not yet in school, until she left her home to be married, Sarah was regularly emotionally, physically, and sexually abused by her father, sometimes on a daily basis. There was ongoing physical violence toward all the family members, including her mother. The everyday family dynamics involved threats, betrayal, and pitting one sibling against the others in order to maintain power and control. In an effort to avoid her husband's angry demands, Sarah's mother sometimes handed her over to her father so that she herself would be left alone. There were few places on their large acreage where Sarah could safely hide from her father. The only certainty in her home was that violence would occur. Everything else was unpredictable.

Sarah's father was an evil man who piously attended his conservative church with his family every week, ensuring that no one would suspect the terror of their life together.

In her late teens, Sarah left the farm, married a good man, and began to raise her own family. Their contact with her family of origin was only occasional. Her parents' home was still not a place of safety. As the reality of her past intruded more and more into her everyday life, Sarah entered counseling. As she began to face the harm that had been done to her, she also came face-to-face with the love of Jesus. Slowly but surely, she opened her heart to the reality of God's grace. She began to trust God and others. Amazingly, over time, she grew in her recognition of and repentance for the sinfulness of her own heart, because we are never only victims, we are also sinners ourselves. Sarah asked God to forgive her sins and God brought profound change to her. She grew in faith; she learned how to love others in the power of God's grace. She changed as a wife, a mother, a friend, and even a daughter. Fantasies of revenge and murder were replaced by a desire for her father to know the gospel. She was able to weep in sorrow, not only for how her father had harmed her, but also for the hardness and evil in his heart.

Years passed and Sarah heard that her father had been diagnosed with leukemia. As his death approached, she began to think about visiting him. She wanted to tell him about what God had done in her heart. She wanted to offer him forgiveness, to express her concern for his soul, and to lovingly call him to repent.

She planned her visit carefully and bathed it in prayer. She went accompanied by her husband and her father's pastor. She went for her father's sake with a heart that had renounced revenge.

There was some small talk and then she told her father plainly and without malice that she remembered how he had harmed her, her mother, and her siblings. She also told him that she loved him and that she forgave him. His response was simply to say harshly that he had probably made some mistakes but there was nothing to talk about. He scolded her because she never came to see him. Her tenderness and tears did not break him. He did not confess his sin or repent of the damage he had done. In fact, while he demanded that she continue to visit him, he mocked her to her siblings after she left and handwrote a note ensuring that she would receive nothing from his extensive estate.

But Sarah, still deeply troubled about his heart, decided to make one more visit to him. This time she went with her husband but without her father's pastor. Without any restraining influence, her father was angry, mean, and destructive. As she looked into his eyes, she saw the reality of his evil and the hatred of his heart because she had exposed his façade. It was a mocking, chilling look that she found hard to forget. After she left, she took her broken heart to Jesus who, like Sarah, had seen the cruel, evil stares of men bent on his destruction.

A few months later, Sarah's father died. At his funeral hundreds of church members, business acquaintances, and relatives paid their respects to a cruel, mean, abusive, evil man. Very few knew the reality of his life or the pain he had caused. As Sarah accepted the condolences of person after person, she was caught in a swirl of disorienting grief. As they watched people file by the casket, her mother asked Sarah, "Don't they know? Why don't they know who he really was? How can so many people think he was a nice man when he was just the opposite?" The ones who did know, other family members, refused to acknowledge what they had seen, heard, or experienced.

There was no justice in this life for Sarah. There was no change in her father, no acceptance of responsibility. She was left to "commit her cause to the one who judges justly." Except for her mother, her siblings and extended family refused to admit the reality of their father's life because they feared it would impact their status in the community. Sarah was alone in facing the reality.

The graveside service was only for extended family. With a dramatic flair, Sarah's sister suggested that each family member write on the coffin with a magic marker some word of remembrance about his or her father, grandfather, uncle, or brother. Some wrote the name they used for him, some wrote complimentary phrases, but no one wrote the truth because to do so would disturb the way the family was perceived. Some of them knew exactly what he was like, but that is not what they wrote on the coffin. Desperately, Sarah began to ask God what to do. After many others had filed past the coffin, writing names they had called her father or events they remembered, she stepped forward, leaned over, and wrote one word on the casket: "Forgiven."

The impact of Sarah's father—his anger, rage, violence, and abuse—went unacknowledged by all except Sarah. Sarah gave testimony to the path she had chosen when she acknowledged the evil done to her. And though her hand shook as she wrote, I believe she was saying with Joseph, "You meant evil against me, but God meant it for good." Her choice brought life to her, to her marriage, and to her children. Joseph remarked that many others would live as a result of his brothers' choice. Sarah's choice opened the door to freedom to any in her extended family who were willing to engage, though no one did.

Perhaps the words of Dan Allender are the best summary for this chapter. When asked about what one may ultimately hope for in the process of redemption, Dan responded:

> "That one day they'll be able to look at their wounds and scars and be able to bless them, always grieving, always bearing some anger, but also knowing that 'You meant it for evil, but God meant it for good.' That they'll be able to hold the paradox of longing for reconciliation while recognizing if it's not possible . . . That they'll learn to truly forgive but also not fall into a false and cheap forgiveness."[4]

I think that Joseph embraced this paradox of forgiveness and lived it out all of his days. Listen to Joseph's words again from Genesis 50:20: "You meant evil against me, but God meant it for good." Then, still holding out sweet redemption after years in Egypt, he tenderly says to his brothers, "'So do not fear, I will provide for you and your little ones.' Thus he comforted them and spoke kindly to them."

Questions for Reflection

1. What seems impossible to you about Joseph's story? How about Sarah's story?
2. What do you think would be the hardest thing about forgiving something that seems unforgivable?
3. What fears would you have to face?
4. What might be exposed about your own heart in the process?
5. What seems to be the most impossible step you may have to take as you think about forgiving someone?
6. The Psalms give us words to describe our suffering and pain, our struggle with evildoers, and our questions about the destruction caused by evil. They also give us hope that God hears our cries and is at work in our struggles. Read through Psalm 10 and answer the following questions:
    - How does it describe evildoers?
    - How does it express your own struggle with evil?
    - How does it point to God's response to evildoers? Understanding these things can guide our hearts, our emotions, and our choices as we wrestle with the challenge of forgiveness.
    - How does it give you hope?

CHAPTER 8

The Cost of Not Forgiving

Susan's mother was getting older and needed daily care. Somehow, even though Susan had three siblings, she was the one who did all of the caregiving. She loved her mother and didn't mind taking care of her, but she did often wish that her two brothers and one sister would lend a hand. Things got worse when Susan's daughter announced her engagement. Now Susan really needed someone to step in and help with her mom so that she could be involved in the excitement of the wedding planning. Despite asking many times, none of her siblings would commit to helping, so she had to hire a caregiver for her mom. Susan began to get angry, then resentful. Since her siblings made no effort to help her, she stopped making an effort to invite them over or be around them. Gradually she cut off all ties with her family. Now it was just her and her mom. Susan didn't care if she ever saw her siblings again.

≈ ≈ ≈

We've seen that forgiving things that seem unforgivable is not easy. It has a cost as we absorb the debt that is owed to us. And to forgive almost always means that we are reminded again of our own need for forgiveness. This is humbling, but it leads us to a deeper trust in Christ and a reliance on him to forgive the one who hurt us.

Sometimes the pain that accompanies forgiveness makes us forget that a failure to forgive has costs of its own. Beth Hunter, in her study guide, *Forgive and Live,* describes what it is like:

> Our hearts tell us that unforgiveness is our friend, but Scripture tells us that it is our worst enemy. It does not give us power but weakens us, making us vulnerable to spiritual enemies who wound and destroy. Unforgiveness does not protect us. It hardens our hearts to God and to others we love, thus keeping them at a distance and leaving us cold, lonely and afraid.[1]

The Root of Bitterness

Scripture often talks about what happens when we hold on to an unforgiving spirit. One result is bitterness. Hebrews 12:15 tells us, "See to it that no one fails to obtain the grace of God; that no 'root of bitterness' springs up and causes trouble, and by it many become defiled."

In Jesus's parable in Matthew 18, the unforgiving servant's heart is untouched by the grace and mercy of the king. He seems blind to his need and how much he has been forgiven. In the face of such amazing forgiveness, he appears to have a sense of entitlement and pride as he vengefully demands payment of a tiny debt owed to him. In fact, he chokes the one who owes him and, refusing to be merciful, throws the man into prison. How could someone who had been forgiven so much do such a thing?

Sometimes when I reread this passage, I am stunned by the unforgiving servant's action. It's hard to even imagine what he was thinking as he dealt with the other servant. But we are the same. The Great King has offered us forgiveness for all our sins, yet we still are easily angered when others do to us what we have done to them or someone else.

Not that you've thrown someone in prison, but perhaps you've spoken a word that reveals anger, hardness, or contempt. You hear it after you said it, but you didn't even know those feelings were there until you heard the words out loud.

The Results of Not Forgiving

There are some outcomes of an unforgiving spirit that are important for us to understand. Unforgiveness is not neutral or benign. It is a destructive, virulent virus that causes much damage and is highly contagious. Bitterness is the result of a settled attitude of unforgiveness over a period of time. Hebrews 12:15 says that not obtaining God's grace may lead to bitterness; it has the potential to "defile" us. Bitterness is not simply remembering a wrong (many wrongs are impossible to forget). Instead, it's making a lasting decision to not offer forgiveness for that wrong. In Ephesians 4:31, Paul describes bitterness alongside "wrath and anger and clamor and slander" and "all malice." These are words strong enough to make us wince because bitterness is a powerful and destructive attitude of the heart.

Itzhak Zuckerman was a hero in the Resistance against the Nazis in World War II, and one of the few survivors of the Warsaw ghetto uprising. Zuckerman was recognized as a hero for his efforts, but his heroism gave him little comfort. After the war, he began a long, dark journey into the depths of alcoholism. Before his death many years later, he talked earnestly and honestly with an interviewer about the bitterness in his soul. He put it like this: "If you could lick my heart, it would poison you."[2]

That quote feels both familiar and terrifying to me. I know that when I don't forgive, my heart becomes so filled with poison that it is a lethal weapon instead of an instrument of God's love.

Unlike Zuckerman, who suffered a great deal, my bitterness can arise in response to small offenses, like when I've been left out of something, or when someone's offhand comment leads me to (perhaps unintended) shame. Then I find myself in a cycle of cynicism, contempt, and criticism. My heart grows cold. There is unbelief, judgment, and the despising of others. Sometimes I don't even want to be rescued.

When we refuse to forgive, we end up being consumed by our focus on the one who has harmed us. We imagine what we would say to her, the harm we want to do in return or wish someone else would do. We live in bitterness, resentment, and bondage. This is what happened to Susan. Although her family certainly did wrong her (and her mother), she was harming herself by not forgiving them. She was the one who was bitter, angry, and resentful. She was the one who had lost her joy in caring for her mom. Her lack of forgiveness did harm to her and to her relationships.

In her book, *Traveling Mercies: Some Thoughts on Faith*, author Anne Lamott says succinctly, "Not forgiving is like drinking rat poison and then waiting for the rat to die."[3]

The unforgiving servant in Matthew 18 leaves us with the question, "Who are you choking with your refusal to forgive?" Perhaps you believe that you are no longer pushing hard against the person's windpipe—"Oh, I'm not choking anyone"—but you know very well that your hands are still around the person's neck, ready to squeeze hard if something else happens. When we have been hurt, it can leave us feeling powerless. We may use our imagination to think of ways to retaliate that compensate for our sense of being trapped or not knowing how to respond. Though we may never carry out these drastic plans, we are still impacted by a heart that toys with revenge, believing that the outcome of our fantasy will provide satisfaction. We miss the truth that the result is, instead, injury to our own heart.

Untouched by Mercy

The unforgiving servant was completely untouched by the king's kindness and blind to the mercy extended to him. Instead, he was filled with resentment and a sense of entitlement. He lost the ability to see himself or others rightly. Is there anyone you are choking by your refusal to forgive?

What was the warning Jesus gave?

Then his master summoned him and said to him, "You wicked servant! I forgave you all that debt because you pleaded with me. And should not you have had mercy on your fellow servant, as I had mercy on you?" And in anger his master delivered him to the jailers, until he should pay all his debt. So also my heavenly Father will do to every one of you, if you do not forgive your brother from your heart. (Matthew 18:32–35)

The prison of unforgiveness is a lonely place, where there is

- no passion for holiness
- no passion for God's glory
- no passion to love others.

Consequences

Our refusal to forgive lands us in prison where there are not only emotional but physical effects directly connected to an unforgiving spirit. Anxiety, depression, and physical illness are a few examples. And that bitter root continues to grow, squeezing life from us.

Dr. Michael S. Barry, Director of Pastoral Care at Cancer Treatment Centers of America in Philadelphia, has written a book entitled *The Forgiveness Project*. After extensive medical, theological, and sociological research, Dr. Barry made a startling discovery. Our immune system is challenged and dysfunctional when our hearts are filled with negative emotions. There are specific physical outcomes in a failure to forgive. It's not surprising that anger has an impact on our bodies. But numbness—which we will experience if we put aside the need to forgive—also has a huge impact. And though forgiveness does not cure cancer, Dr. Barry tells the stories of a number of cancer patients who came to healing and peace after learning to forgive. We are fearfully and wonderfully made!

There may be other outcomes or consequences to holding a grudge or refusing to forgive. We certainly will begin to experience some relational distance from others. Our heart is holding on to a mean and perhaps even violent secret as we toy with hatred. One result is that in order to ensure that others do not discover what is locked away in our heart, we will begin to live in fear of being truly known, and emotional and perhaps even physical intimacy in relationships will be significantly impaired. We may find ourselves beginning to live in isolation, though on a superficial level that may not be observable at all.

Questions for Reflection

Look again at this quote from Beth Hunter:

Our hearts tell us that unforgiveness is our friend, but Scripture tells us that it is our worst enemy. It does not give us power but weakens us, making us vulnerable to spiritual enemies who wound and destroy. Unforgiveness does not protect us. It hardens our hearts to God and to others we love, thus keeping them at a distance and leaving us cold, lonely and afraid.

1. What do you think she is describing when she says unforgiveness feels like a friend?
2. How might we think that not forgiving could protect us?
3. Do you often find yourself thinking of what you might have said or done to retaliate against someone who has hurt you?
4. Think of a person you need to forgive. Is there bitterness in your heart toward this person? (Bitterness is not the same as remembering how you were harmed, though bitterness may lead you to obsess over what happened.)
5. Is there anything going on in your body that could be related to bitterness or a lack of forgiveness? (Headaches, digestive problems, muscle pain, fatigue, depression? Almost every bodily system can be impacted by the stress of not forgiving.)

CHAPTER 9

Some Things Forgiveness Is Not

Forgiveness can be a painful, challenging process, as we have seen. It is also something God calls us to as his forgiven children. It shows us our own need for forgiveness and binds our hearts to him for the strength and faith to forgive.

Sometimes, however, forgiveness can be made needlessly more painful and difficult because we have misunderstood what it involves. This chapter will discuss some of those misconceptions and offer a more biblical perspective.

Forgiveness Is Not the Same as Denial

When we need to forgive someone, it is often difficult to acknowledge the extent of the debt the person owes us. Just facing it can involve grief, pain, and loss. So perhaps it isn't surprising that we sometimes choose to say that we aren't bothered by what happened, or we completely deny that it happened, or we continue to insist that the person who harmed us was "just a good person who made a mistake."

As a counselor I have often sat with wounded men and women who are trying to put the pieces of their life together. I've listened to them talk about someone who deliberately harmed them, beat them, or violated them. Perhaps the person had been unfaithful to them or abandoned them, or was cruel and mean in a judgmental or self-righteous way.

Yet in words like these, here is what they say:

"She didn't really mean it."

"They aren't that bad, actually."

"He's really a good person underneath."

John grew up in a family where shame, rage, and humiliation were all part of being together. He was often the target of degrading humor from family members who seemed to enjoy working as a tag team to target some small mistake of John's that had been uncovered. His father's words and actions toward John, his mother, and his siblings were particularly mean and cruel.

John's family of origin was a war zone. But if you asked John about his family, he would list his father's impressive accomplishments: a success in local politics, dinners with national political figures, an established family business, a comfortable financial situation that included a vacation home, friends in important places, parties that everyone enjoyed. Attending an evangelical church was a weekly occurrence as well as a place where the father held a prominent position. No one in the family ever talked about the "covert war" where hostilities were displayed on a regular basis. No one spoke about the fear that ruled their interactions. Certainly the abuse and contempt with which his mother and his siblings were treated was never mentioned.

Years later, the good news of the gospel and a long period of excellent counseling began to lift the impact of denial from John's heart. It was not an easy process because it involved facing a reality that the entire family had conspired to keep secret. But refusing denial brought freedom and joy to John and others in his family.

Denial is a powerful weapon that allows evil to continue. A response of denial comes from hearts that fear acknowledging the enormity of harm, especially when it occurs with a cloak of normality. In my case, it was desperately difficult to admit that the kindness I initially enjoyed from my abuser was part of his strategic plan to seduce me. But I had to face it to move forward. Forgiveness is not about denying what actually happened.

Forgiveness Is Not Trying to Feel Good About Something Wrong or Evil

In his book, *Healing the Wounded Heart*, Dan Allender has this to say: "Evil's primary way of operating is in darkness and secrecy, subtly using its cunning to reach its ultimate goal: ruining the glory of God."[1]

Like John, you may be uncomfortable putting actual words to the reality of harm that has been done to you. But moving toward forgiveness does not mean an absence of anger at sin or minimizing the reality of harm that is involved. If "evil operates in darkness and secrecy," as Allender describes, then, as God's children, we are called to walk in the light by clearly describing what harm has come to us. Forgiveness cannot move forward if we are trying to minimize wrong or evil. Over and over God calls evil exactly what it is as a way of bringing it into the light.

In Luke 7, even as Jesus offers forgiveness to the sinful woman who washed his feet with her tears and poured expensive ointment over them, Jesus says to her and then to Simon, "Her sins, which are many, are forgiven" (Luke 7:47). If sin is not clearly described, the forgiveness is diminished. We do not have to feel good about something that is wrong, but we cannot ignore the reality of evil.

Scripture doesn't mince words when it comes to sinful behavior for any of us. In 1 Corinthians 6:9-11, Paul compiles a list of sinful choices and is quite direct about it, mentioning the sexually immoral, idolaters, adulterers, those who practice homosexuality, thieves, the greedy, drunkards, revilers, and swindlers. He says that those who live like this will not inherit the kingdom of God.

The beauty of this passage is not Paul's acknowledgment that such people exist, but that some of the Corinthian believers had *been* those kinds of people. Being blunt and direct about their evil behavior makes his next sentence jump off the page.

"But you were washed, you were sanctified, you were justified in the name of the Lord Jesus Christ and by the Spirit of our God." You were like that!

One reason we need to be real about how we have been hurt is that we are all self-deceivers. When we minimize wrong done to us, it harms our hearts because we know the hurt is greater than we have stated. It also harms the heart of the perpetrator, who is not given the chance to see the truth about the damage she has done. Seeing and hearing what really happened is the only way that Christ can help that person bring it all to him for forgiveness and cleansing.

Forgiving Is Not the Same as Forgetting

How many times have you heard someone say, "Forgive and forget"? It is true that Jeremiah 31:34 tells us that a time is coming when God will no longer "remember" our sins. Micah 7:19 also says that God is a God who pardons iniquity, and "will cast all our sins into the depths of the sea." Psalm 103:12 tells us that God has removed our transgressions from us as far as the east is from the west. All of these passages use metaphor to help our minds and hearts understand that our sin is so well covered in the atonement Jesus provides that they are hidden or put away. God's love for his people is so filled with compassion that it leads him to put our sin where it will never be seen or heard about again.

But though we are made in the image of this gracious, pardoning God, we are unable to control our thoughts or memories in this way. Does that mean we have not forgiven? Does forgiveness equal forgetfulness, as we are sometimes told? Dan Allender comments:

> Both pictures of forgiveness—forgetfulness and distance—are metaphors that are not to be literally

93

mimicked in our life. Imagine trying to find the spot where East and West are farthest apart to deposit another's transgression against us in that place. Literally forgetting the harm done to us would be as difficult as finding that geographical point. The only way to do so would be through unbiblical denial. Obviously, holding on to a memory for the purpose of demanding redress or justifying the hateful distance is not biblical either. Biblical forgiveness, however, is not minimization or forgetfulness.[2]

Forgetting is not how we forgive, nor is it a test of forgiving. We remember because we are made in the image of a God who remembers. It is an important part of his image in us.

So remembering does not mean that we have not forgiven. But remembering may remind us that there is more to forgive, or it may show us that hardness and bitterness have taken hold of our hearts and we need to repent for that. In either case, we find ourselves in a place where we need God's mercy and grace.

But that is a good place to be. Remembering may lead you to celebrate God's mercy that you are forgiven and that God has given you grace to forgive. Few things are sweeter than being with someone from whom you were once estranged and realizing that it is all right, it is safe, to again come face-to-face with each other.

It is interesting that in both the Old and New Testaments God ordained a liturgy of remembrance to remind his people of his love and care for them. Passover was instituted as a memorial to God's saving power as he rescued the Israelites from the hand of the Egyptians. The liturgy of the Seder begins with this question, which is recited by the youngest person at the table capable of reciting it: "Why is this night different from all other nights?"

Even now around the world, Jewish people stop to remember the wonder of God's intervention that led them out of slavery and safely through the sea to begin a new life. In order to memorialize what God did on their behalf, they have to acknowledge the harm from which they were rescued.

As Christians, we have also a liturgy of thanksgiving and rescue as we come together to share the Lord's Supper. As we eat and drink the bread and the wine, we remember the body and blood of the Lord Jesus given for us. But in order to remember, we too must call to mind the suffering of Christ on our behalf; how the Lamb of God, in whom was no sin, suffered, died, and was resurrected so that we might experience redemption. All around the world, Christians from every tribe and nation are invited to join in keeping the Feast of Redemption.

God wants us to remember because, as we embrace the bread and the wine, we come face-to-face once more with the reality of our hearts and our need for a Savior. I have been in communion services where the pastor offers the elements with the words, "Come and eat and drink. You need this."

We are called to remember because with the remembrance comes again the reality of our need for forgiveness and God's sweet gift as he meets that need. Forgiveness is not the same thing as forgetting.

Forgiveness Is Not Simply a One-time Event

Many times we think, "But I still remember what happened and how painful it was. I guess I haven't forgiven after all."

Offering forgiveness does not guarantee that from that point on, you will not remember what happened. Forgiveness is often a process because sin has long-term impact. Years may pass and the damage of sin may resurface, its effects felt all over again. After forty years, I returned to the geographic area where my abuse occurred. Many memories flooded my mind and brought a lot of distress. I was reminded of how young and vulnerable I was when it happened and that, because of where it occurred, I should have been safe. At that point, I had to forgive another time, both the past wrong and the present damage. I may need to forgive one event seventy times seven.

If, when you remember, your heart becomes angry and filled with bitterness, then the Holy Spirit is graciously calling you to let go of the hardness gripping your heart.

But perhaps you remember and your heart is saddened not only by what was done, but by genuine concern for the person who harmed you. That is the voice of the Spirit reminding you to pray that God will call her heart to repentance as well.

In a wonderful book called *Yearning*, author Craig Barnes reminds us that God has broken into our world to pursue us, but he does not promise to paste us together in this life and give us wholeness. Barnes says instead, "What God wants to give us is Himself. If we really believed that, it would be enough. In fact, it would be more than enough. It would overwhelm us."[3]

God is not so much interested in fixing us as he is in restoring us to a dependency on him. It is often only in the broken parts of our lives that we actually begin to desire what he wants to give us . . . himself. God's call is for us to live by faith in the power of the gospel for today rather than live trapped under a personal resolve to "never remember again."

Forgiveness Is Not Contingent on Another's Repentance. It Is about My Heart Before God.

My abuser died before I understood that what had happened was sexual abuse. I never spoke with him about it or heard him repent. But I still needed to forgive him.

Lewis Smedes writes, "Forgiveness happens only in the mind and heart of someone who has been wronged. It is an event in the spirit of the offended person that lays the groundwork for and creates the opportunity for reunion of two people."[4] Smedes also indicates that because forgiveness is an internal process in the heart of the one who forgives, it is possible that the one who has been forgiven may never know it has happened.

It may seem strange that our forgiveness might not directly involve the person being forgiven. But this is because the command to forgive comes from God, and the power and motivation to forgive flow directly from the forgiveness we have received from him through Christ. Just as the king was offended by the unmerciful servant's failure to forgive a fellow servant, our failure to forgive after we have been forgiven is a matter between us and God, even more than it is between us and the other person. God's concern is with the state of our hearts.

Think of how often you may need to forgive a roommate, a close friend, a spouse, or family member.

- We can forgive before there is resolution.
- We can forgive when there is no resolution.
- We can forgive tons of things without ever saying anything because love covers a multitude of sins (James 5:20).

Forgiveness Is Not about Forgiving Ourselves

When forgiveness is discussed, people often ask, "What if I can't forgive myself?" It is a complicated question and a difficult one to answer because those who ask often feel somewhat tormented by what they perceive to be their own guilt.

As we forgive, it may be true that we have to face the evil of our own heart that is exposed, as well as the evil of the offender's heart. We have already looked at places where hidden rage may surface. Hatred for the one who harmed us may be a part of the process of acknowledging the harm that has been done to us. There are many ways for our hearts to harden until we feel we are beyond the point of forgiveness. There we may begin to believe that we cannot forgive ourselves.

So what help is there if we find ourselves in this dilemma? I believe this is a difficult situation, but I also believe that we need to be careful when we put ourselves in a place that is beyond

God's forgiveness. I wonder if lurking under the burden of "I can't forgive myself" may not be a deep sense of pride, or our fear that what we have done is more than God is able to manage. Both fear and pride are weapons of the Enemy, who continues to tell us that God cannot be trusted, that God is not enough, that God demands something more than receiving his forgiveness. When this happens, we believe that we can somehow fix things even though we are worthless and powerless. It might make sense that the only way is to "forgive" ourselves.

But we already know that God is able to offer us a complete pardon because of Christ. Perhaps our first step out of the dilemma is to be realistic in our evaluation of our own sinfulness. Our tendency might be to minimize the true condition of our hearts because it has the potential to become a difficult struggle or because our hearts are sad about the harm we have experienced. Living with the torment of how we might have failed or the guilt that haunts us is surely a weapon of the Enemy. Jesus stands with open arms, inviting us to come to him. The wounds he bears give testimony to our forgiveness even when we don't feel forgiven. There is real peace and joy offered to us even when we have failed. There is no need to go on doing battle when the fight is finished.

This old hymn helps us to remember the extent of the mercy God offers us.

> There's a wideness in God's mercy,
> Like the wideness of the sea;
> There's a kindness in his justice,
> Which is more than liberty.
>
> There is welcome for the sinner,
> And more graces for the good;
> There is mercy with the Savior;
> There is healing in his blood.

There is no place where earth's sorrows
Are more felt than in heaven,
There is no place where earth's failings
Have such kind judgment given.

There is plentiful redemption
In the blood that has been shed;
There is joy for all the members
In the sorrows of the Head.

For the love of God is broader
Than the measure of man's mind;
And the heart of the Eternal
Is most wonderfully kind.

If our love were but more simple,
We should take him at his Word;
And our lives would be all sunshine
In the sweetness of our Lord.[5]

It is interesting to google self-forgiveness or "Forgiving Ourselves." There are pages of articles, books, and information that discuss this problem. Many of them say that you are worth forgiving, so stop being so hard on yourself. Many writers promise freedom and even abundance if you simply decide to "let go" of whatever you are using against yourself and move on. At first glance, not very many writers discuss any need for personal forgiveness from God.

For those who struggle to forgive themselves, there is a caution that is important. Our own effort is not what brings us forgiveness. And none of us are beyond the boundaries of God's unambiguous and indisputable offer of forgiveness. When we say we cannot forgive ourselves, we may be standing in a place that refutes the truth of God's offer. It is almost as though we are saying that we are somehow better recordkeepers than God is, or that the redemption Christ gave his life to provide isn't enough because we are such huge sinners.

If you struggle with this problem, do you find yourself wondering, "Is God's mercy enough for someone like me?" God's offer of mercy is unfailing and if we begin to believe that we are beyond his offer of mercy, though we may appear sad, helpless, and in pain, I want to say with all kindness, "Do you really believe you are too much for God? Do you think that the cross of Christ does not cover whatever you hold against yourself?" Please be careful, because our Enemy is not beyond luring us into a place where we feel disconnected, lost, and too much for God to handle. But it may be a false humility, even a kind of pride that is hidden behind such despair. God's offer of forgiveness is open to all who believe, no matter what they have done or left undone. You are not beyond God's reach even if your heart continues to tell you that you are. If you struggle with accusations against your own heart, realize that the Enemy is inviting you to deny God's saving grace. Satan is clever, because it is not a denial that you have done something wrong; it is a denial that God has done what is necessary to cover that wrong.

Each one of us is sweetly invited to:

> Come ye sinners, poor and needy,
> Weak and wounded, sick and sore;
> Jesus ready stands to save you,
> Full of pity, love and power.[6]

For those of us walking with someone struggling with this problem, we can come alongside with the kindness and gentleness of the Savior to help them see again the fullness of God's mercy and grace, to them and to us.

Forgiveness Is Not a Guarantee That the Person Will Repent

When we offer forgiveness to someone, it may lead to conviction of sin, repentance, and reconciliation. It may also lead to a hardened heart, more denial, an intensification of sin, and even greater division. That was Sarah's experience in chapter 7.

We are not in control of the outcome nor are we responsible for it. We only need to answer God's call to our own hearts to forgive. Paul writes in 2 Corinthians 2:15–16, "We are the aroma of Christ to God among those who are being saved and among those who are perishing, to one a fragrance from death to death, to the other a fragrance from life to life."

Forgiveness Is Not the Same as Reconciliation

> And Samuel did not see Saul again until the day of his death, but Samuel grieved over Saul. And the LORD regretted that he had made Saul king over Israel. (1 Samuel 15:35)

Samuel had confronted Saul about a serious sin and Saul had not repented. Samuel mourned for Saul for the rest of his life, but he never saw him again. Paul's confrontation with Alexander did not lead to reconciliation either.

> Alexander the coppersmith did me great harm; the Lord will repay him according to his deeds. Beware of him yourself, for he strongly opposed our message. (2 Timothy 4:14–15)

In order for a relationship to be reconciled and restored, there must be a rebuilding of trust, based on grace from the one harmed and radical repentance on the part of the offender.

Deep repentance rarely presents itself in an instant. It is more often evidenced over time in a change of heart and behavior. Unfortunately, many offenders want to be forgiven without a process of repentance and visible change. They want to say, "I'm sorry," sometimes without even acknowledging what they are sorry about, just to be done with the process. But that is not repentance and it does not lead to meaningful reconciliation.

We talked in chapter 6 about renouncing revenge, but that does not mean that there are no consequences for the damage done by the offender, especially when there is no repentance. When Paul wrote to Timothy about Alexander the coppersmith, Paul had forgiven Alexander and entrusted him to the just judge. ("The Lord will repay him according to his deeds.") But he nonetheless makes it clear that Timothy should be cautious in his dealings with him. Forgiveness is not the same thing as reconciliation.

Reconciliation requires a work of God in the heart of the offender. Sometimes reconciliation does not occur at all. Even when it does, it may require a long time and the intervention of many persons. But when it happens, it is a taste of glory!

Questions for Reflection

1. Reread the chapter and make a list of all of the things that forgiveness is not. Are there any that are a new thought for you? Which ones?
2. Which categories in this chapter are the most difficult for you and why?
3. Choose at least two categories listed in question #1, and write briefly about how they might help you in a situation where you find it hard to forgive. You are writing a case study of your own heart. No one else needs to read it, so be honest and trust the Holy Spirit to encourage your heart in the process.

CHAPTER 10

Everyday Forgiveness

How do we usually use the word "everyday"? Doesn't it usually refer to a task that must be repeated again and again? Almost all "daily" things have the potential to become boring or to seem like drudgery. They are normal, familiar, routine.

Forgiveness is something that we usually need to do daily. But "everyday forgiveness" is never ordinary, because it's remarkable anytime forgiveness is offered.

When we studied the Lord's Prayer in chapter 2, we read these words: "Forgive us our debts, as we also have forgiven our debtors" (Matthew 6:12). In his pattern for prayer, Jesus mentions things we might pray about daily, and he includes forgiveness as part of the normal rhythm of life. As sure as we need to eat every day, so we will need to forgive and be forgiven.

The Breath of Forgiveness

As we follow Jesus's example, we will keep short accounts with God and with one another. We will live expecting that we will need to be forgiven and that we will need to forgive. Daily we need to breathe in God's forgiveness of us and breathe out our forgiveness of others.

Taking a deliberate, slow breath often helps us focus. On the edge of my laptop is a small stone that says "breathe." It helps me to sit back, relax, and realize that whatever I am feeling so intensely can be put on hold for a moment to give my body time to relax.

Just to remind you of how regular and simple day-to-day forgiveness is meant to be, take a deep breath in . . . and now let it out. The next time you struggle to forgive an everyday occurrence, take a deep breath of God's forgiveness and let out a deep breath of your forgiveness toward others.

Dealing with Daily Irritants

What daily annoyances do you often have to deal with? Here are a few possibilities.

- Do you have friends/family who are often or always late? Does it irritate you, especially because you are someone who arrives on time?
- Do you have friends/family/coworkers who are arrogant, defensive, critical, or angry and you don't like what they do (even though you can justify those things in yourself)?
- Are you impatient with your coworker, your roommate, your children, your spouse because they don't manage themselves in the excellent way you do?

If we say that we really don't need to forgive in situations like these (we can just "overlook"), we must ask ourselves if we are actually extending grace to the person or sweeping something under the rug because of denial or a fear of conflict.

The things that bother us every day are usually about our time, about having our space, about order vs. spontaneity, about saving money or spending it, about how we like things done or left undone. You know what your list looks like. Do you more often forgive in these categories or need to be forgiven?

We might have other questions about everyday, "normal" forgiveness. For example, Are there some things you don't have to forgive? Shouldn't we just overlook some things? Do we deal with daily irritants differently than we do bigger events?

Isn't the answer both "yes" and "no"?

Let's look at Ephesians 4:29–5:2, where Paul is talking about those daily irritants.

> Let no corrupting talk come out of your mouths, but only such as is good for building up, as fits the occasion, that it may give grace to those who hear. And do not grieve the Holy Spirit of God, by whom you were sealed for the day of redemption. Let all bitterness and wrath and anger and clamor and slander be put away from you, along with all malice. Be kind to one another, tender-hearted, forgiving one another, as God in Christ forgave you. Therefore be imitators of God, as beloved children. And walk in love, as Christ loved us and gave himself up for us, a fragrant offering and sacrifice to God.

What are the don'ts?

> Don't use foul, abusive, or "corrupting" language.
> Get rid of bitterness, wrath, anger, clamor, slander, and malice.

And what are we to do?

> Let your words build each other up and bring grace to those who hear them.
> Be kind, tenderhearted, forgiving as God in Christ forgave you.

The do's and don'ts in this passage describe how God wants us to live with one another. But almost immediately it becomes a description of what we fail to do . . . every day. As soon as we read these words, our inability to do what is described becomes readily apparent. And we fail at this not just daily, but perhaps many times each day.

If this describes me and it describes you as individuals, what do you think will happen when we get together? Every day, we will do things to each other that lead us to believe that the *real* everyday irritants in life are you and me.

In this passage, Paul reiterates Jesus's words in the Lord's Prayer: "Be kind to one another, tenderhearted, *forgiving one another as God in Christ forgave you*" (v. 32, emphasis mine). *The Message* paraphrase says, "Forgive as quickly and as thoroughly as God in Christ forgave you."

This is a quick transaction of the heart, but we all know that it's not automatic. Perhaps the idea of breathing in and breathing out makes even more sense here, helping our hearts to remember our need for the power of the Spirit to shape whatever we breathe out.

What Does Forgiveness Look Like?

What does this daily process of forgiveness look like? "How" do we do this? What is it like to walk along this path?

In Luke 17:1–5, Jesus was talking with the disciples about spiritual temptation. He said,

Temptations to sin are sure to come, but woe to the one through whom they come! It would be better for him if a millstone were hung around his neck and he were cast into the sea than that he should cause one of these little ones to sin. Pay attention to yourselves! If your brother sins, rebuke him, and if he repents, forgive him, and if he sins against you seven times in the day, and turns to you seven times, saying, "I repent," you must forgive him. The apostles said to the Lord, "Increase our faith!"

The disciples knew right away that what Jesus was asking of them was more than they could simply "decide" to do. Jesus was speaking to them about stumbling blocks or temptations to sin.

We live in a fallen world, so there will be times, places, and events in your life when people will sin against you, and times when you will sin against others. We are dangerous people because we have sinful hearts. We are good at "out-sinning" others. We do this when we complain about something someone has said about us and surreptitiously invite the person listening to be critical too. When we correct our children with anger or coldness, our heart attitude is often worse than the child's offense. We criticize, judge, and yell at our roommates or spouses for the way they have treated us until we have done far more damage than they did originally.

When we have been wronged, we feel that a response equal to the wrong is justified. "If you cut in front of me, I won't let you merge. If you came late to lunch last week, don't be upset when I'm late for coffee today. If you were mean to me yesterday, I can be annoyed with you this morning." When someone hurts me, I automatically feel that I have something on him or her. I feel free to judge them and justify myself.

Pay Attention to Yourself

In Luke 17, Jesus reminds the disciples that temptations to sin will come but we need to "pay attention" to ourselves so that they do not come through us. One way we need to "pay attention to" ourselves when someone hurts us is to be aware of that first impulse to separate ourselves from that person. We distance ourselves. It is an automatic response of the heart because if you hurt me, I want to get far away from you so I won't have to think about it and you won't be able to do it again. I want to make a gap between us and to feel good about it. So I make a list of what you have done wrong and I tell myself that I would never do what you have done. What are some ways in which you need to "pay attention to yourself" when someone hurts you?

When someone has harmed us, we may feel uncovered and shamed, so we go in search of a covering. In Genesis 3, as soon as Adam and Eve disobeyed God's command, the text says, "They knew that they were naked" (v. 7). Now, they had been naked all along, and Genesis is careful to record that. But until then, they felt no shame being naked in each other's presence or in God's. Now, suddenly, they have to cover up and hide from God.

Come Out of Hiding

We have not come far from Genesis 3. When we sin in word or deed, we usually find some way to run for cover. The fastest way for me to cover myself is by comparison. I remind myself of my own righteousness and I rehearse what you do that I don't. I ignore what I have done wrong and go over my list of things I've done right. I make myself righteous based on your unrighteousness. In that moment, I turn away from the covering Jesus gave his life to give me. Instead, I am covered in fig leaves of self-righteousness.

Are there things that you almost always do or almost never do in your relationships? Be careful—they can quickly become a covering for the places you fail. I can easily tell you all the things you've done that I would never do, and fail to see the ways in which I am just like you.

In her book, *Redeeming Eve,* Heather Webb says,

If you are like me, you have known moments of being alienated but you have also been guilty of alienating others. In overcoming the discomfort of dealing with someone I do not understand, I can make them an Other and thereby dismiss them. Others are used as scapegoats, to unite a group against a common enemy, to give a sense of worth over and above someone else or to find an excuse for why life doesn't work.[1]

Doesn't it make more and more sense why Jesus warned the disciples, "Pay attention to yourselves"? Look at your own heart. Ask God to show you how you are like the person who has just spoken to you rudely, no matter how different you may feel. Right here you will need an infusion of God's grace, because when we are hurt, we find it extremely difficult to examine our own heart.

Speak Truth about Yourself and Others

I don't want to pay attention to myself. I want all eyes to be on the one who hurt me. I want that person isolated, condemned, judged, and certainly not forgiven. Most of all, I want everyone to know that I would never act the way she acted. I so easily forget that yesterday I did the same kind of thing.

If someone tells me a lie, in my heart I call them a liar. It's black and white, clear and simple. He did not tell the truth. I don't remember that yesterday I (note the words I use) distorted, rearranged, and refocused to cover up the truth. In reality, I *lied* yesterday to cover up why I was late to a meeting, or to look good in front of someone—but I tell myself that it's not because I am a liar. I am just a complicated person who isn't completely truthful.

Miraslov Volf in the book, *Spacious Heart*, says, "Forgiveness flounders because I exclude the enemy from the community of humans and I exclude myself from the community of sinners."[2]

Jesus also makes this point. It is your brother or your sister—a fellow human, a fellow image-bearer of God—who has sinned against you. So if you pay attention to yourself and ask the Holy Spirit to show you your heart, soon (much sooner than you would like) you will discover the times that you lie. God will kindly bring to mind your self-righteous judgment against the one who lied to you.

Pursue Your Brother and Your Sister

In the Luke 17 passage, Jesus includes another, perhaps even more difficult step to the forgiveness process. Being willing to release and forgive the person may include going to him. You have to be willing to be in an uncomfortable reality. He is your brother and he has done something wrong. Jesus says, "If your brother sins, rebuke him and if he repents, forgive him," even if it happens seven times.

Why do you think Jesus requires this? Jesus is moving us in the opposite direction from the one we would most likely choose. He says we should be going toward the person . . . on purpose . . . for a purpose.

This process moves us out of denial and helps us to face reality. It forces us to carefully articulate our understanding of what has happened. When we have been hurt, we are not immediately good about doing either of these things.

Have you ever needed to go to someone about something she did to you? What process did you go through? You would need to calm down, to think clearly, to find words to describe what happened and how it impacted you.

What usually happens is quite different. When we are hurt, we lash out or shut down. We get angry; we separate ourselves from the offender and begin developing our case against them.

Here is Jesus's simple remedy:

1. Look to your own heart and your own record.
2. Make sure you see the person as your sister or your brother, another sinful human being, just like you.
3. Take the next step of speaking to him.

What a great way to deal with roommates, friends, church members and families!

It may also be a powerful way to approach our enemies!

Jesus's words convict us. And there are other helpful Scriptures as well. Peter tells us in 1 Peter 4:8 that "love covers a multitude of sins." And James 1:19 reminds us that as we follow Jesus's words, we are also to "Be quick to hear, slow to speak, slow to anger." Paul says, "Restore . . . in a spirit of gentleness" (Galatians 6:1). Jesus has told us to reach out to our brother and the other writers remind us of the heart attitude we need as we go.

We all have different first-response emotions. Some of us flee and some of us fight. Jesus calls out both kinds of persons. If you are one who flees, you need to go to the offender. You are called out of silence and you will need God's grace and the Spirit's power to be brave enough to speak. If you react by fighting, you are called to go, not as an enemy, but as a brother. You also need God's grace to go with tenderness and concern, seeing yourself as the same kind of sinner.

Forgiveness as a Lifestyle

There is one other small comment in the Luke 17 passage to consider. Jesus says that if your brother sins against you seven times in one day, you should forgive him seven times. Because of Jesus's interaction with Peter about how many times we are to forgive, I'm pretty sure that the number is not the issue. It is our willingness to persevere with someone when there is conflict. But Jesus is also reminding us that forgiveness is to be offered over and over again. We need it all the time and we need to offer it all the time. It is a lifestyle.

Should we ever overlook things? Of course. But overlooking does not mean that we minimize them or pretend they didn't happen. Overlooking is more like an unarticulated forgiveness. You are giving someone an anonymous gift—no one knows but you. It is not an action that earns me righteousness and significance. It is not an action that allows me to be proud of my obedience. It is an action that simply recognizes that before the day is out, I will need the same forgiveness.

It is very encouraging that the disciples come back to Jesus in Luke 17 and say, "Increase our faith." They knew that on their own they would not be able to do what Jesus was describing. And you and I know that as well.

But we have a heavenly Father who loves us, a Savior who gave his life to ransom us, and the Holy Spirit who lives in our hearts to counsel and encourage us. And that is more than enough.

Questions for Reflection

1. Sometimes there are patterns in our lives that we have not considered to be sinful. Are there any behaviors in your life that others close to you have asked you to change? Perhaps thoughts, words, and actions that you have previously put in the category of "everyone does that." What are they? If you are unable to think of any, ask your spouse, children, roommate, or best friend.

2. Suppose you are willing to overlook a sin that is often committed by someone close to you. Is it helpful or harmful to do so? Why or why not?

3. Make a short list of things that irritate you on a regular basis. Now ask someone who knows you well to tell you what things irritate you. Are the lists similar? Ask the same person what it is like for them when you become irritated. If you live with small children, ask them to draw a picture of how you look when you are irritated.

4. Take a few moments to ask the Holy Spirit what the underlying sin is in your day-to-day patterns of irritation.

5. Write a few sentences about how you would like to change and how that change might come about. If you really don't know how to change, or don't want to, ask the Holy Spirit to help you understand what is blocking that good desire.

CHAPTER 11

Forgiveness, Worship, and the Growing Kingdom of God

After the resurrection, Jesus speaks with his followers in Luke 24. Verse 45 tells us that he had opened their minds to understand the Scripture. Then in verses 46–47 he says, "Thus it is written, that the Christ should suffer and on the third day rise from the dead, and that repentance and forgiveness of sins should be proclaimed in his name to all nations, beginning from Jerusalem." In Acts 1 he tells them how this will happen.

> But you will receive power when the Holy Spirit has come upon you, and you will be my witnesses in Jerusalem and in all Judea and Samaria, and to the end of the earth. (Acts 1:8)

Who is to carry this message? Jesus's audience was made up of fishermen, tax collectors, prostitutes, and ordinary people. The one unifying fact about them was that they had received forgiveness for their sins from Jesus. And in what must have been a huge disruption for them, Jesus tells them that they will now take the good news of the gospel to Jerusalem, Judea, Samaria, and the ends of the earth, to all the nations. They may have begun sharing the message locally, but Jesus was clear that they were to travel far and wide so that everyone should hear.

Following the King's Command

The gospel message that goes to all nations includes the forgiveness of sins. Our sins are forgiven! We are good with that part of the gospel. But it goes further to teach us that we are to "forgive as God has forgiven you," that he will "forgive us our debts as we forgive our debtors."

Needing forgiveness and offering forgiveness are not optional. Learning how to breathe in forgiveness for ourselves and breathe out forgiveness for others may be complicated. It may take time. It may require forgiving seventy times seven, but for the sake of our own hearts and for the sake of the world to which we are sent, forgiveness is a place God calls us to go. It is a necessity.

As believers in Christ, we live under the reign of a King, and sometimes the news that forgiveness is not optional seems a bit threatening. But remember where we began in Matthew 18, when we looked at the story of the good-hearted king. He forgave a huge debt by paying it with his own money. He was kind and gracious to a servant who could never pay him back.

But remember this as well. What was his response to the same servant when he refused to forgive? The king threw him into prison. Why?

The point of Jesus's parable is not that we will go to hell if we struggle to forgive others. He is warning that if we refuse to forgive and instead demand justice from others, it reveals that we have never availed ourselves of the mercy and forgiveness that God offers us. The unforgiving servant did not embrace the mercy and forgiveness that the king offered him. He did not see his true need or the extravagant grace that the king had extended. Perhaps it was pride or a sense of entitlement; perhaps he told himself that he deserved the money he'd owed, or that someday, with enough time, he would repay the debt. We aren't told, but what is clear from the parable is that he was not humbled, grateful, or changed by the king's mercy. We know that because he did not extend mercy to the servant with the much smaller debt.

When you stand before the Great King and truly receive mercy, forgiveness, life, and grace, then grace and forgiveness fill your life. You will pass it on to others. But if we demand justice from others, we are refusing the mercy and forgiveness of God. We will suffer the due punishment for our sins, because we have rejected the only remedy there is. We have spurned the offer of the tenderhearted king and chosen to rely instead on our own record. We have rejected the gospel.

We have considered how patient and compassionate God is with us in regard to forgiving and how we need to extend that compassion to others who are struggling. But there *is* a bottom line: We are called to forgive.

The Supernatural Source of Forgiveness

Humanly speaking, forgiveness is impossible, but that is when we must remember that it does not begin with us. It begins with God. His generous forgiveness, which cost him so much, was not offered because we deserved it, but because he is a gracious, loving, and merciful God. When we are humbled to see our need and gratefully accept that forgiveness, we are changed by that transaction with God. Our relationship with God is restored and our hearts are filled with love, gratitude, worship, and a desire to serve the God who loved and forgave us. Out of that reservoir of grace and mercy, God enables us even to forgive the unforgivable, though in ourselves that would be impossible. But God often invites us to be part of something impossible, and then he does the impossible through us.

Forgiveness *requires* that supernatural intervention! If you think it is easy, either you are in denial or you have never been deeply hurt. It requires a supernatural change in our hearts. But the gospel has the power to change us in unimaginable ways.

A few years ago Laura Hillenbrand told the story of Louis Zamperini, an Olympic runner, in the book *Unbroken*. When World War II broke out, he joined the Air Force and fought against the Japanese in the Pacific until his Air Force bomber crashed into the Pacific. One of the few survivors, Louis struggled to a life raft and pulled himself on board.

Zamperini and his friends were rescued by the people they had sworn to fight, the Japanese. Taken to a prisoner of war camp, Zamperini soon became a target for the commanding officer, Watanabe, and his henchman called The Bird. They were determined to break a prisoner who was physically strong and willing to stand against the evil that the camp directed toward himself and other prisoners. Zamperini and others were deprived of food, sleep, clothes, and most of all their dignity. Watanbe's goal was to leave them broken and dehumanized.

After a long and terrible time, Zamperini was rescued and returned to America. It was not an easy adjustment. It is no surprise that his reentry was a time of enormous personal suffering for Zamperini. He no longer fit in the place he called home or as a citizen of the country where he lived. As he struggled with post-traumatic stress disorder, his life spiraled out of control into rage, fear, and bitterness.

One evening, Zamperini heard Billy Graham speak about how God asks of us only the faith to believe in him. Louis took Graham's invitation to heart, became a Christian, and slowly started his long road back. He felt profound peace. When he thought back on his history, what resonated with him was not all that he suffered but the divine love that had intervened to save him. He no longer believed he was a worthless, broken, and forsaken man. His rage, fear, humiliation, and helplessness began to change. He was a new creation.

Following his conversion he began to work with troubled boys, using outdoor environments to grow their courage, physical strength, and understanding of themselves. He told them his story as well as the way he had found peace with God.

Later in his life, Louis visited the prison where he had been held and heard that The Bird had died. Previously he had written a letter to the Bird and to Watanabe. When Watanabe received the letter asking him to meet with Louis, he spit on the letter, crumpled it on the ground and stomped on it. After some time, Louis heard that Watanabe had died.

On January 30, 1998, an article appeared entitled, "Olympic Torch Relay Rekindles Ex-POW's Flame of Forgiveness." Louis had been given an opportunity to carry the Olympic torch in Japan. He was almost eighty-one years old. He could no longer run the way he had in the past, but he raised the torch and began running. All around him were smiling Japanese faces. There were men who had worked beside him as a prisoner and 120 Japanese soldiers formed into columns to let him pass. The cages were long gone, only the cheering of voices, some falling snow, and an old, yet joyful man, running.

Zamperini's story shows us the power of God to sustain, heal, and change someone who has been broken by terrible treatment at the hands of others. It also shows us the power of a life poured out for others in service and ongoing forgiveness.

How Worship Moves Us toward Forgiveness

How do our hearts move toward a desire to forgive? I think worship takes us there. Worship is the experience of having my heart broken in God's presence over what I have done and what I have left undone. Worship is the place where my deep selfishness is confronted and exposed by Christ's deep selflessness. Consider these words from *The Book of Common Prayer*:

Most merciful God,
we confess that we have sinned against thee,
in thought, word and deed,
by what we have done,
and by what we have left undone.[1]

We are sometimes willing to come to God to confess what we have done, but how often do we confess that what we have *not* done reveals our lack of love for God and for others?

William Temple, archbishop of Canterbury from 1942-1944, wrote this definition of worship:

> Worship is the submission of all our nature to God. It is the quickening of conscience by his holiness; the nourishment of the mind with his truth; the purifying of imagination by his beauty; the opening of the heart to his love, the surrender of will to his purpose—and this gathered up in adoration, the most selfless purpose of which our nature is capable and therefore the chief remedy for that self-centeredness which is our original sin and the source of all actual sin.[2]

Gratitude Leads to Worship

In Luke 7, we meet a sinful woman who interrupted a dinner party to anoint Jesus's feet with her tears and the ointment from an alabaster jar. Jesus used her as an example that stunned the religious leaders when he said, "Therefore I tell you, her sins, which are many, are forgiven—for she loved much. But he who is forgiven little, loves little" (Luke 7:47).

She knew she was a debtor, and it turned the way she looked at the world upside down. Suddenly a life's earnings could be poured out simply to honor Jesus. It cost her in the moment because she looked foolish and knew she would be shamed. It cost her for the rest of her life because the ointment was probably her life savings. But she paid the cost willingly because her heart was broken by her sin and filled with gratitude for the forgiveness Jesus extended to her.

Her sacrifice started with the fact that she knew she was in need of forgiveness and her heart melted when she received it. The process of forgiveness always begins where we stand empty-handed before the cross, with no defense or covering for our shame unless we receive the righteousness that comes from Christ's atoning death. Worship then flows from a grateful heart, a heart filled with awe, a heart that stands amazed by the forgiveness of the good-hearted King.

Worship puts life into perspective. It is a return to sanity, where the true order of the universe is made clear. We are the creatures; he is the Creator. And the cross, where the cost of forgiveness can be observed, stands at the center of this universe, shining with the glory of God.

When we worship, we understand that we are the servant in Matthew 18 who is unable to pay, the servant at the mercy of the good King, in need of grace. As we worship, we also realize that the moral gulf between us and those who owe *us* a debt is not that huge.

How does worship bring these things together?

- We remember what the unmerciful servant forgot: We have nothing.
- We are empty-handed as we face the million-dollar debt required by God's justice—and what does God do? He cancels the debt.
- He endured the suffering that should have been ours to pay our debt.
- When we are powerless, having nothing, and terrified by how much we owe, we can look into the eyes of the

One we owe and see that our debt has been cancelled. We are safe.

That experience of powerlessness opens our hearts to forgive others—and to be willing to experience the powerlessness that accompanies extending forgiveness. That is, when we forgive, we surrender our right to demand something of those who owe us.

Forgiveness, Joy, and Grace

Instead, in forgiveness, we give others the grace that has been given to us. Forgiveness is what we are able to offer when we read that the Father delights in us—that he sings over us with joy as we read in Zephaniah 3:14–17:

> Sing aloud, O daughter of Zion;
>   shout, O Israel!
> Rejoice and exult with all your heart,
>   O daughter of Jerusalem!
> 15 The Lord has taken away the judgments against you;
>   he has cleared away your enemies.
> The King of Israel, the Lord, is in your midst;
>   you shall never again fear evil.
> 16 On that day it shall be said to Jerusalem:
> "Fear not, O Zion;
>   let not your hands grow weak.
> 17 The Lord your God is in your midst,
>   a mighty one who will save;
> he will rejoice over you with gladness;
>   he will quiet you by his love;
> he will exult over you with loud singing."

God not only takes away our punishment and offers us forgiveness, he rejoices over us with "loud singing" and "quiets" us with his love. He is a God who can dance, sing, and rejoice, but who also can comfort and quiet our weary hearts with his love. This kind of worship softens even the hardest heart.

Worship is an experience that will enable you to move through:

Pain, denial, anger, protest, sadness,
Renouncing revenge, canceling the debt,
Repenting again of an unforgiving heart,
Facing evil for the sake of good,
Speaking truth from a kind and careful heart
Living with a heart that longs for change in the one who harmed you.

Worship will remind you again that we forgive because we have been forgiven.

Forgiving Like the Father

In Rembrandt's famous painting of the prodigal son returning to his father, the son has a shaved head, one of his shoes has fallen off, and his clothes are rags. He is kneeling before his father, with his head on his father's chest. The father, wearing a beautiful red cape, has his hands tenderly placed on the prodigal's back.

There are three other men in the picture; it may be the older brother who is barely visible in the darkness. The story in Luke 15 is a story of reunion and blessing, a story of love offered to two brothers, each with a different response.

When we read the story, we tend to identify either with the prodigal or the older brother. And we assume that the father is a picture of our heavenly Father. Of course that is true, but not to the exclusion of realizing that we are called to be like the father, as well as like the prodigal.

Jesus told this story to Pharisees, tax collectors, sinners, and teachers of the law. In New Testament culture, teachers of the law belonged in the "righteous" group and tax collectors and sinners were part of the "unrighteous" group. While Jesus was exposing to his audience the tendencies of their own hearts, he was also describing the heart of his Father. In Rembrandt's picture, the father is receiving the lost son, but Luke tells us that the father had been watching for his son, and saw him when he was "a long way off" (Luke 15:20).

What does that say to us as we think of those we need to forgive? Are you willing to wait for the one who wronged you, hoping for his repentance? Has your heart ever been impacted by what it is like for him to live in the pigpen?

Can you imagine yourself standing in the road, waiting for him to come back to God? Do you allow yourself to imagine what he would be like if God empowered him to repent?

Battles of the Heart

Think of some things that might prevent your heart from becoming like the heart of the father. There are a number of things that might keep you from desiring the person's redemption:

Anger

Pain

Revenge

No one knows how much you have been hurt

No one has seen your suffering

I went through a dark time a few winters ago. I had been sick a couple of times and, in addition to being housebound, I had other annoying problems that didn't seem solvable at the time. I really felt that God should change my circumstances and end the suffering in my life. My self-talk was "I deserve better than this."

Then, through the Holy Spirit's mercy, I began to remember that while God made no promise of pain relief, there was hope for a rescue from my heart's responses.

I wrote in my journal:

I don't want to embrace this deliverance because the process exposes the reality of my heart where there is bitterness, anger, fear, resentment, self-pity, offense, and hopelessness in the crucible of present pain and suffering. But I am forgetting that the exposure of my heart takes me back to the gospel where there is redemption for the very things I am trying to hide by keeping a stiff upper lip.

Isn't it a little interesting that desperation often precedes deliverance? Sometimes facing the hard reality that we need to be delivered, a reality that involves a revelation of the sad condition of our heart, is a major step toward healing.

When our hearts are hard and dark, we generally want pain relief. But God wants us to come to him and again acknowledge our dependence on what he offers. He wants us to be receivers of the gospel, again and again. His mercies are continually new.

Paul Tripp says it well in his devotional book, *New Morning Mercies*.

> God's mercies never grow old. They never run out. They never are ill-timed. They never dry up. They never grow weak. They never get weary. They never fail to meet the need. They never disappoint. They never, ever fail, because they really are new every morning. Form-fitted for the challenges, disappointments, sufferings, temptations, and struggles with sin within and without are the mercies of our Lord.[3]

One of the things that surprised me most in my recovery process was that I didn't really know how change came about. When heart change happens, there is an internal shift that doesn't come from something I do. It comes from what the Holy Spirit does, and it can't be explained any other way. It is truly God's mercy that has tunneled its way into the depths of my heart.

When we suffer, we want to be acknowledged and recognized as worthy and valuable. And when suffering results in our losing the recognition of others, we default into self-pity—poor me! But during that time, we miss the One who is waiting in the road, inviting us to a celebration.

Standing at the Cross

Do you have a heart that is willing to forgive? Stand at the cross of Christ and look again at how much you have been forgiven. Do you find the cross a boring place? Do you find its familiarity numbing? Look again—and while you look, ask the Holy Spirit to show you the ugly sinfulness of your heart, not in the past, but right now. What's been going on in your heart in the last twenty-four hours that was part of the debt Jesus paid?

You may be able to control your behavior when you are surrounded by others, but sometime today you have needed forgiveness from the good-hearted King because of the anger, bitterness, demand, criticism, or selfishness that is in your heart.

How are you like the one you need to forgive? This is the radical message of the Kingdom:

- "Be compassionate as your Father is compassionate."
- "Forgive as you have been forgiven."

Often our immediate response is, "When will so-and-so be compassionate to me?" But that is when the Spirit reminds us of who God has made us to be and what he promises us.

The Spirit himself bears witness with our spirit that we are children of God, and if children, then heirs—heirs of God and fellow heirs with Christ, provided we suffer with him in order that we may also be glorified with him. (Romans 8:16)

We are to inherit all that the Father owns. Are you ready for this inheritance? Jesus said it looks like this:

You're blessed when you're at the end of your rope. With less of you there is more of God and his rule.

You're blessed when you feel you've lost what is most dear to you. Only then can you be embraced by the One most dear to you.

You're blessed when you're content with just who you are—no more, no less. That's the moment you find yourselves proud owners of everything that can't be bought.

You're blessed when you've worked up a good appetite for God. He's food and drink in the best meal you'll ever eat.

You're blessed when you care. At the moment of being "care-full," you find yourselves cared for.

You're blessed when you get your inside world—your mind and heart—put right. Then you can see God in the outside world.

You're blessed when you can show people how to cooperate instead of compete or fight. That's when you discover who you really are, and your place in God's family.

You're blessed when your commitment to God provokes persecution. The persecution drives you even deeper into God's kingdom.

Not only that—count yourselves blessed every time people put you down or throw you out or speak lies about you to discredit me. What it means is that the truth is too close for comfort and they are uncomfortable. You can be glad when that happens—give a cheer, even!—for though they don't like it, *I* do! And all heaven applauds. And know that you are in good company. My prophets and witnesses have always gotten into this kind of trouble. (Matthew 5:3-12 MSG)

The Power of Kingdom Love

I think that sometimes we fear the nature of kingdom love and kingdom loving. It is not the inclination of our hearts to live and love with the kind of abandonment Jesus showed to us. Our hearts are most often inclined in the opposite direction. It is not the kind of loving and living we can do because we try harder or because we experience some moral reformation. It is a lifestyle requiring personal spiritual transformation.

That is why Jesus has gone before us, to make that transformation possible. Jesus gave up everything. Philippians tells us that he even refused to hold onto something that was already his—equality with God.

He humbled himself and became obedient. Hebrews says that "he learned obedience through what he suffered" (Hebrews 5:8). And his worst suffering was not physical. He took the wrath of God against sin and bore it for us. He who had no sin became sin for us so that we might become his righteousness (2 Corinthians 5:21)! Is that amazing?

Someone who needed no forgiveness has made a way for us to become like him!

We forgive because we have been forgiven. Forgiveness cannot be coerced or dragged out of us. It is only the love of Christ that compels us.

Coming Home

Offering forgiveness is a call to others to come home, but it is a call to the forgiver as well. What does *home* mean to you? Perhaps it includes things like safety, acceptance, welcome, love, joy, family, play, rest?

You know how your heart longs for rest. You know how you long for the hardness in your heart to be softened. You know how the weight of your unforgiving heart is too heavy to carry anymore.

Come home!!!

The Father will throw a party. The angels will rejoice. And you will find the grace to invite others to join you in the Father's house. Every invitation will look somewhat different, but every invitation will look like the Father's invitation to us.

Face-to-Face

You may already know the story of Jacob and Esau's reunion in Genesis 33. Years before, Jacob had cheated his brother out of his birthright and his blessing from their father. The brothers had gone their separate ways, unable to work out their differences.

Now, years later, Jacob was returning to his home country and preparing to encounter Esau for the first time. Jacob knew that his brother was preparing to meet him, and Jacob was afraid. He gathered up many gifts for Esau and sent his servants, his children, his wives, and the rest of his retinue across the River Jabbok ahead of him, because he didn't know what he would face when Esau arrived. He wanted Esau to meet them first and perhaps be softened by the encounter.

However, after everyone else had left, Jacob spent a lonely night wrestling with an unknown man (who turned out to be God) and won. The man changed Jacob's name to Israel, "for you have striven with God . . . and have prevailed" (Genesis 32:28). Jacob responds, "I have seen God face to face, and yet my life has been delivered" (v. 30).

When the sun rose and Jacob began his journey again, he looked up and saw Esau coming toward him with four hundred men. When Esau saw Jacob, he ran to meet him. He embraced him and fell on his neck and kissed him, and they wept. Then Jacob said, "I have seen your face, which is like seeing the face of God, and you have accepted me. Please accept my blessing that is brought to you, because God has dealt graciously with me" (Genesis 33:10–11).

God's face toward us is always favorable because of Jesus. Where might God call you to show his face to others?

Think of the person you need to forgive. Ask God to impress upon your heart a way you can choose to love the person who has harmed you. You have an opportunity to show that person the face of God. What might that look like?

Does it seem impossible? Consider these words of John Bunyan:[4]

RUN JOHN RUN the law commands,
But gives us neither feet nor hands.
Far better news the gospel brings,
It bids us fly and gives us wings.

My prayer and hope is that the gospel will give you wings to fly to Jesus, to receive the forgiveness that is in the gospel again and again for your own heart, in such a way that you cannot wait to fly to those you need to forgive with that same sweet message. This is God's promise and calling for all who have been changed by Jesus. May you experience the gospel joy and freedom that forgiveness brings!

Questions for Reflection

1. What is the initial response of your heart when you hear that we forgive because we have been forgiven?
2. What are some of the things we might experience when we find it hard to forgive? Which of these words might describe you?
3. Using this prayer from the *Book of Common Prayer* as a model, write a prayer in your own words, asking God to

forgive a recent or ongoing sin. The prayer describes this as "what we have done."

> Most merciful God,
> we confess that we have sinned against thee
> in thought, word, and deed,
> by what we have done,
> and by what we have left undone.[5]

4. Now write another prayer using this model, talking about a recent time when you did not do something you knew you needed to do, something you "have left undone."
5. Imagine yourself standing before the cross. What is your heart's response?
6. Perhaps there is a situation in your life where you stand as the father of a prodigal person, watching and waiting for someone to "come home." What is it like to wait and watch for this person's return? What do you hope to experience?

Endnotes

Chapter 1

1. I am indebted to Pastor Scotty Smith for elements of this summary.

2. J. R. R. Tolkien, *The Two Towers* (New York: Ballantine Books, 1965), 283.

Chapter 2

1. Timothy Keller, *The Freedom of Self-Forgetfulness* (Farrington Leyland, England: 10Publishing, 2012), 5.

2. Keller, *Freedom of Self-Forgetfulness*, 38–39.

3. Keller, *Freedom of Self-Forgetfulness*, 39.

4. Keller, *Freedom of Self-Forgetfulness*, 38.

5. "Ransom." *Merriam-Webster.com*. Merriam-Webster, n.d. Web. 4 Apr. 2016.

Chapter 3

1. John R. W. Stott, *The Cross of Christ* (Downers Grove, IL: InterVarsity Press, 1986), 67.

2. This list is adapted from material presented by Timothy Keller, pastor of Redeemer Presbyterian Church, New York.

Chapter 4

1. Augustus M. Toplady, "Rock of Ages," 1776.

Chapter 5

1. Diane Langberg, "Suffering and the Heart of God," in *by Faith*, March 2016, 32–37.

2. Dan B. Allender and Tremper Longman, *The Cry of the Soul* (Colorado Springs: Navpress, 1994), 66.

Chapter 6

1. John Roach, "Brain Study Shows Why Revenge Is Sweet," National Geographic News, http://news.nationalgeographic.com/news/2004/08/0827_040827_punishment.html; and Brian Knutson, "Sweet Revenge?" *Science* 305, no. 5688 (August 27, 2004): 1246–47, http://www.sciencemag.org.

2. J. R. R. Tolkien, *The Return of the King* (New York: Ballantine Books, 1965), 284.

3. Maltbie D. Babcock, "This Is My Father's World," 1901.

Chapter 7

1. C. S. Lewis, *The Lion, the Witch and the Wardrobe* (New York: HarperTrophy, 1978), 86.

2. Derek Kidner, *Genesis: An Introduction and Commentary* (London: Tyndale Press, 1967), 68.

3. Lewis B. Smedes, *Forgive and Forget* (San Francisco: Harper, 1984), 141.

4. Dan Allender, quoted in "Forgiving the Unforgivable? Shame, Silence and Sexual Abuse" by Joy Beth Smith, *Today's Christian Woman*, March 2016.

Chapter 8

1. Beth Hunter, *Forgive and Live* (Brenigsville, PA: Xulon Press, 2003), 17.

2. Itzhak Zuckerman, "Reflections on the Holocaust," http://kids.brittanica.com/holocaust/article-9078476.

3. Anne Lamott, *Traveling Mercies: Some Thoughts on Faith* (New York: Pantheon Books, 1999), 134.

Chapter 9

1. Dan B. Allender, *Healing the Wounded Heart* (Grand Rapids: Baker Books, 2016), 35.
2. Dan B. Allender, *The Wounded Heart* (Colorado Springs: Navpress, 1990), 222.
3. M. Craig Barnes, *Yearning* (Downers Grove, IL: InterVarsity Press, 1991), 18.
4. Lewis B. Smedes, *The Art of Forgiving* (Nashville: Moorings, The Ballantine Publishing Group, Random House), 59.
5. Frederick W. Faber, "There's a Wideness in God's Mercy," 1862.
6. Joseph Hart, "Come Ye Sinners," 1759.

Chapter 10

1. Heather P. Webb, *Redeeming Eve* (Grand Rapids: Baker Books, 2002), 55.
2. Miraslov Volf with Judith M. Gundry-Volf, *The Spacious Heart* (Harrisburg: Trinity Press International, 1997), 57.

Chapter 11

1. Church of England, *The Book of common prayer with the additions and deviations proposed in 1928* (Cambridge: University Press, 1960), Holy Eucharist, Rite 1.
2. William Temple, *Readings in St. John's Gospel. 2 vols.* (London: MacMillan, 1945), 1939–1940.
3. Paul David Tripp, "Introduction," *New Morning Mercies* (Wheaton, Ill.: Crossway Books, 2014).
4. Attributed to John Bunyan (1628–1688).
5. Church of England, *Book of common prayer*, Holy Eucharist, Rite 1.

mission
propelled by good news

At Serge we believe that mission begins through the gospel of Jesus Christ bringing God's grace into the lives of believers. This good news also sustains and empowers us to cross nations and cultures to bring the gospel of grace to those whom God is calling to himself.

As a cross-denominational, reformed, sending agency with more than 200 missionaries and 25 teams in 5 continents, we are always looking for people who are ready to take the next step in sharing Christ, through:

- **Short-term Teams**: One- to two-week trips oriented around serving overseas ministries while equipping the local church for mission

- **Internships:** Eight-week to nine-month opportunities to learn about missions through serving with our overseas ministry teams

- **Apprenticeships:** Intensive 12–24 month training and ministry opportunities for those discerning their call to cross-cultural ministry

- **Career:** One- to five-year appointments designed to nurture you for a lifetime of ministry

 Grace at the Fray   **Visit us online at: serge.org/mission**

spiritual renewal resources for you

Disciples who are motivated and empowered by grace to reach out to a broken world are handmade, not mass-produced. Serge intentionally grows disciples through curriculum, discipleship experiences, and training programs.

Resources for Every Stage of Growth

Serge offers grace-based, gospel-centered studies for every stage of the Christian journey. Every level of our materials focuses on essential aspects of how the Spirit transforms and motivates us through the gospel of Jesus Christ.

- **101**: The Gospel-Centered Series
  Gospel-centered studies on Christian growth, community, work, parenting, and more.
- **201**: The Gospel Transformation Series
  These studies go a step deeper into gospel transformation, involve homework and more in-depth Bible study
- **301**: The Sonship Course and Serge Individual Mentoring

Mentored Sonship

For more than 25 years Serge has been discipling ministry leaders around the world through our Sonship course to help them experience the freedom and joy of having the gospel transform every part of their lives. A personal discipler will help you apply what you are learning to the daily struggles and situations you face, as well as, model what a gospel-centered faith looks and feels like.

Discipler Training Course

Serge's Discipler Training Course helps you gain biblical understanding and practical wisdom you need to disciple others so they experience substantive, lasting growth in their lives. Available for onsite training or via distance learning, our training programs are ideal for ministry leaders, small group leaders or those seeking to grow in their ability to disciple effectively.

 Grace at the Fray

Find more resources at serge.org